Prophets

Isaiah–Malachi

Leg 4

08 09 10 11 12 13 14 15 16 17—10 9 8 7 6 5 4 3 2 1

Cover Design: Keely Moore

Contents

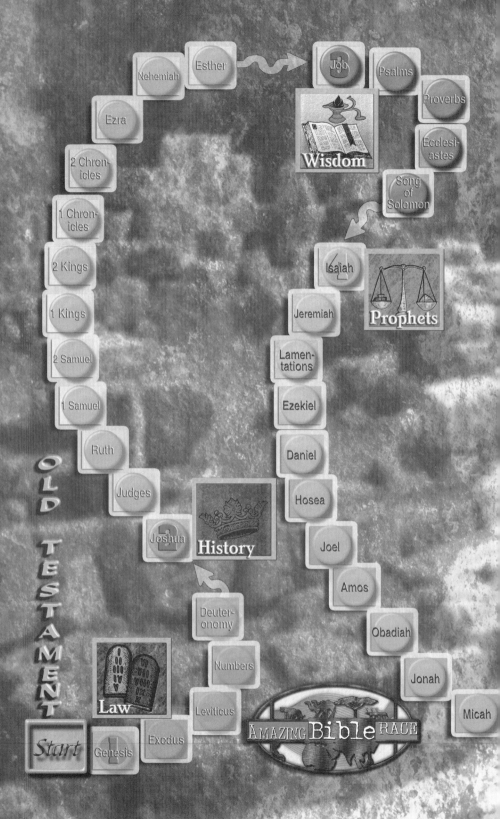

Early Church

John

Luke

Mark

Matthew

Gospels

NEW TESTAMENT

Acts

Romans

1 Corinthians

2 Corinthians

Galatians

Ephesians

Philippians

Colossians

1 Thessalonians

2 Thessalonians

1 Timothy

2 Timothy

Titus

Philemon

Hebrews

James

1 Peter

2 Peter

1 John

2 John

3 John

Jude

Prophecy

Malachi

Zechariah

Haggai

Zephaniah

Habakkuk

Nahum

Letters

Finish

Revelation

© 2007 by Abingdon Press

At the Halfway Mark

Congratulations on making it to Leg 4 of the Amazing Bible Race. You're now halfway through. Since you've read half of the Bible, you might as well read the rest, right? So far you've learned about hundreds of laws, met dozens of judges and kings, and experienced timeless wisdom. Now you'll hear from some of the most interesting folk in history: the prophets of Israel and Judah. The prophets might drive you crazy sometimes, but that's just a part of their job.

As you continue the Race, keep a few things in mind:

1. **Be a team player**—Teamwork is an important part of the Amazing Bible Race; it will help you get through difficult passages and hurdles. Don't be afraid to ask for help from a teammate and be willing to offer *your* help to your teammates.

2. **Give it your all**—If you ever become discouraged or overwhelmed, just think about how far you've come and how much you've learned. Keep digging and keep learning. Don't give up!

3. **Focus on the journey, not on the prize**—While the Amazing Bible Race has points, prizes, and a finish line, reading and studying Scripture is a life-long task. The true objective of this Race is not to beat other teams or to win a grand prize but to meet God in Scripture daily and to learn about God's will for the world. Don't get so wrapped up in the competition that you lose sight of what's really important.

4. **Use a Bible translation that you understand**—If you still haven't found a Bible translation that you're comfortable with, try something else. If you'd prefer a Bible written in contemporary language, try the *Contemporary English Version* or *Today's New International Version*. If you're looking for something more scholarly, go with the *New Revised Standard Version* or the *New International Version*. Websites such as *bible.crosswalk.com, www.biblegateway.com,* and *bible.oremus.org* allow you to search within and read from several translations. You might also choose to listen to Scripture on the Internet or on your MP3 player. (For free MP3 files, search key words *free Bible MP3* to locate various free MP3 downloads. Then choose the version that you like best.)

Amazing Bible RACE

The Rules

Rule 1
Follow steps 1–4 for each daily reading.

Rule 2
As a team, answer the Weekly Challenges and submit them to the website.

Rule 3
Accomplish any Fast Forwards that appear in your Runner's Reader. A Fast Forward appears periodically and is a life-application exercise for your team. You'll be asked to find a way to apply the Bible reading to your life. For example, if you're reading about feeding the hungry, you might decide to serve food at a local rescue mission. To receive credit for the outing, you must have someone make a video of it or take a photo of your group in action; then upload it to *amazingbiblerace.com.*

Rule 4
Help your teammates overcome any Hurdles. When you face a particularly difficult section of Scripture or feel that you're getting stuck, you might see a Hurdle. Hurdles allow you to skim that particular Scripture passage and accomplish or perform a task based on the Bible lesson or solve a quiz on *amazingbiblerace.com* to "quiz-out" of that section.

Rule 5
Earn as many points as possible for your team. You gain points by finishing your daily readings, solving Weekly Challenges, participating in the Fast Forwards, solving the extra quizzes, or looking on the map and taking a quiz. The more effort you put in to the Race, the more you'll get out of it—and the more points you'll receive!

Rule 6
The adult mentor is the team coach who keeps team members encouraged and motivated. The coach should check in at least once a week to make sure that everyone is reading and that you have a time scheduled to work together (by IM, e-mail, text message, or phone conversation) to solve the Weekly Challenge.

Rule 7
Support your team and work together.

Rule 8
Have fun!

It's All Going Downhill
Isaiah 1–5

1 Scouting the Terrain

The sections of Isaiah that you'll read this week involve two distinct parts. Chapters 1–12 are God's address to the people of Judah, who are descendants of Jacob and, therefore, God's chosen people.

Trailblazer
• Isaiah

Speaking through Isaiah, God tells the people how they have rebelled against God's Law. The Northern Kingdom of Israel and Southern Kingdom of Judah continue to war, fail to live with justice, and make hollow praises to God. Instead of fully trusting God, they worship idols. God warns that bad things will happen. Nevertheless, God will restore the relationship between God and God's people.

However, God is not only concerned with Judah and Israel. Chapters 13–23 address other kingdoms, including the kingdom of humanity and the kingdom of the sea. All are under God's eye and within God's reach.

• As you read Chapters 1–5, think about how Isaiah might address our world nowadays. How have God's children learned from mistakes of the past? What mistakes are we still making?

• How would you define *justice*? In what ways, do you think, does God call us today to seek justice?

• How are righteousness before God and justice inseparable?

2 NOW READ ISAIAH 1–2.

3 Switchback

God doesn't beat around the bush here, saying, in effect: *Hey, everybody, listen up! I gave Judah everything, and they have stabbed me in the back. They're worse than a bunch of stubborn donkeys who will not listen to their master. But at least a donkey remembers who his master is.* The language at the beginning of the Book of Isaiah makes it clear: God is angry and has good reason to be.

God hates the worship of the people of Israel and Judah because it is not sincere. The people make a big show of worshiping God, then they turn around and violate God's Law by exploiting the poor and the weak. They do not pursue justice. As Isaiah 1:15 puts it, the people's hands are "full of blood."

How do we make sure that our worship is pleasing to God? "Remove the evil of your doings from before my eyes; cease to do evil, learn to do good; seek justice, rescue the oppressed, defend the orphan, plead for the widow" (1:16b-17). We are all called to be more holy. God is ready to forgive a repentant people who want to return to justice and righteousness. Although our "sins are like scarlet, they shall be like snow" (1:18b).

• When or how do your actions conflict with true worship of God?

Road Signs

- **Zion:** The high hill in Jerusalem on which the Temple stood was known as Zion, and the term was sometimes used to refer to Jerusalem and its people as a whole.
- **Sheol:** Jews of Isaiah's day believed that the dead went to Sheol, a limbo-like place of nothingness.

The Book of Isaiah begins with a message of judgment and restoration for God's people. Divide your team into three subteams. Assign each subteam one Scripture section: A. 1:2–2:5; B. 2:6–4:6; or C. 5:1–6:13. For its assigned passage, each subteam should make a list of key terms that speak of God's judgment against Judah and a list of key terms that speak of God's promise to restore God's people. Compare and discuss your lists as a team. Then go to *amazingbiblerace.com* to take a quiz.

 Prayer

God, help us be more holy and help us pursue justice so that we can truly worship you. Amen.

The Man of Unclean Lips
Isaiah 6–10

Scouting the Terrain

The majority of the reading for today is written in a different style from most of the rest of Isaiah. Like a lot of the writings of other prophets, much of Isaiah is poetry. Most of Isaiah 6:1–9:7, however, is narrative; it tells stories. The short stories we read today are glimpses into the life of Isaiah and his call to become a prophet.

Through these stories, we begin to see not only how God calls Isaiah, but also how Isaiah becomes a father, how God tells Isaiah to reassure the king of Judah during a civil war, and how God will ultimately save the people.

Trailblazers

• Isaiah
• King Ahaz of Judah
• Priest Uriah
• Zechariah

• Based on this week's readings, how would you describe Isaiah's overall message?

• What can you tell about Isaiah, based on the glimpses of his personality shown within today's readings?

NOW READ ISAIAH 6–10.

3 Switchback

God calls Isaiah as a prophet but charges him to "make the mind of this people dull, and stop their ears, and shut their eyes, so that they may not look with their eyes, and listen with their ears, and comprehend with their minds." Why wouldn't God want the people to "turn and be healed" (Isaiah 6:9-10)?

Although much of Isaiah's message is about punishment, a clear message of hope remains. Isaiah 7:14 tells of a time when a child shall be born whose name, Immanuel, means "God is with us." He reminds the people that they are not alone. In some ways, God is like a parent who punishes a child for doing something wrong but comforts the child with a hug at the same time.

Isaiah 10:20-27 offers even more reason for hope: a vision of a time when the punishment will end and God will remove the people's burden. This hopeful vision of the future, common within many of the prophets' messages, helps sustain God's people during the roughest times. Vision provides an escape for people who hurt—even if that escape may come only when they close their eyes and dream.

Road Signs

- **Maher-shalal-hash-baz** (MAY-huhr-SHAL-al-HASH-baz) (8:1): This is the longest name of any person in the Bible. It means "the spoil speeds, the prey hastens," which is a reference to the coming destruction of Israel (Samaria) and Syria (Damascus) by Assyria.
- **"Day of Midian"** (9:4): This refers to a great military victory the Israelites won long ago against Midian, which is recorded in Judges 7.

• How have you found hope in the past? How can you give hope to others?

• How can you provide comfort to people and offer a vision of better times?

4 Prayer

God of hope, grant us comfort and vision in our darkest times. Comfort us with your presence. Give us eyes to see your unseen work that is already crafting a greater future. Amen.

Racing Tip

The time about which Isaiah writes in today's section takes place around 736 B.C., right before a three-year war called the Syro-Ephraimite war (735–732 B.C.).

The Power of God's Justice
Isaiah 11–14

1 Scouting the Terrain

Chapters 11–14 continue Isaiah's vision of hope. Here, the vision expands to show how powerful God is and how well God will take care of the descendants of Jacob. As you read through this section, imagine how someone who is poor and oppressed would hear these words. The people for whom Isaiah wrote did not live in the wealthiest country in the world, did not have enough food to eat, and did not have many of the rights that you enjoy.

Imagine that you have barely enough to eat, and you see a few rich people with everything anyone could ever want. Imagine that you cannot vote, say anything bad about the government, or question the injustice of your situation. Imagine that you have seen family members die—some because of starvation, some because of fighting in a war, and others because of the cruelty of soldiers who occupy your land. Imagine that soldiers walk into your house or business whenever they want and can take anything they choose.

- If you were in the impoverished state described above, how, do you think, would you respond to Isaiah's vision? How would it change you?

Trailblazers

- **Isaiah**
- **Messianic king**
- **Philistines**
- **Assyrians**
- **Lions and lambs and other predators and prey**

Pace Pusher

Try reading it out loud:
- 11:2
- 11:6-9

2 NOW READ ISAIAH 11–14.

3 Switchback

The vision of the peaceable kingdom (11:6-9) has captivated people for centuries. It provides an image of wolves and lambs, calves and lions, cows and bears, all living side by side in harmony. Lions, the ultimate carnivores, will eat straw. The promise is not just an end to war but also an end to violence and fear in all of God's creation. When God's justice truly takes over, people and animals will be able to live in the presence of God on earth; for "the earth will be full of the knowledge of the LORD as the waters cover the sea" (11:9b). Knowledge of God will be like the air we breathe. All that we do will be done in our awareness of God.

How do we get there? The journey, or process, will be painful, says Isaiah, like the agony of a woman in childbirth (13:8). After the pain, however, comes peace and joy over the new life.

• Have you ever had a terribly painful experience that, once it was over, was also very rewarding?

Road Signs

• **Ephraim:** The prophets often use this name of this prominent tribe to mean the entire Northern Kingdom of Israel.

• **"The stump of Jesse":** Isaiah prophesies that the righteous ruler to be sent from God will be from the family tree of David, whose father was Jesse.

• **Day Star, Son of Dawn:** Some of the people of Israel worshiped morning stars and other celestial objects as gods.

Racing Tip

Isaiah 14:12-20 warns the king of Babylon, in a mocking tone, of the consequences blasphemy—believing that you can do greater things than God or that you can replace God.

4 Prayer

Rain the knowledge of you, Lord, down upon this earth so that we may dwell together without fear and full of peace. Amen.

The Scope of God's Eye
Isaiah 15–18

① Scouting the Terrain

Chapter 15 begins a new section of Isaiah. Earlier, God pronounces judgment on Israel and Judah. Here, the prophet announces God's judgment on other nations, including Moab, Damascus, Ethiopia, Egypt, Tyre, and others. This section offers a powerful reminder that God attends not only to God's chosen people. All are held to some measure of justice and goodness, regardless of whom they worship or what they believe. God does not judge them because they were born outside of Israel and Judah (something over which they had no control). They are judged because of their wickedness.

Trailblazers

- Isaiah
- Moabites
- People of Damascus

• What does Isaiah tell us about how God holds people accountable?

WEEK 1 ◇ DAY 4

• By what standards does God judge the nations of the earth?

Pace Pusher
Read it out loud:
- 16:2-4
- 17:4-6

② NOW READ ISAIAH 15–18.

3 Switchback

The Moabites and Israelites were long-standing enemies. Yet when Moab is destroyed, God calls for mourning: "Let everyone wail for Moab. Mourn, utterly stricken" (16:7). We do not know exactly why the author would mourn so much over the downfall of an enemy. We can guess, however, that God had hoped that Moab would change its ways. Maybe the prophet sees in Judah the same sins that were in Moab and, therefore, recognizes that Moab's destruction is a lesson for the people of Judah. Perhaps the prophet wants the people to remember that the Moabites are not merely enemies but distant relatives as well (see Genesis 19:37). In any case, the oracle against Moab is a reminder that God is Lord of all people.

Road Signs

- **Moab:** This nation, located across the Dead Sea from Judah, was a traditional enemy.
- **Damascus:** Today, as in Isaiah's time, 2,500 years ago, Damascus was the capital of Syria, northeast of Jerusalem.

God charges the children of God to welcome the Moabites, to give them justice, relief, and comfort. Perhaps this was to be a lesson in forgiveness—that their shared experience of judgment would bring the Israelites and Moabites together. Hospitality shown to the Moabites reveals God's continual effort to forgive and move on. Punishment is not to be eternal. In God's eyes, there is always an opportunity for redemption.

- Whom do you consider your enemies or rivals? Which of these people could use your compassion and comforting?

hurdle Reread chapters 15–18 and make a list of sins for which God is punishing the various nations. Do you see any consistent themes? What sins seem particularly offensive to God? Take a quiz on *amazingbiblerace.com* to check your understanding of these chapters and earn points.

 Prayer

Glorious God, help us comfort the modern-day Moabites in our midst and all of those who have undergone suffering. Amen.

The Wide Reach of God
Isaiah 19–23

1 Scouting the Terrain

Now we come to more pronouncements that show how far-reaching God's command is. God speaks to Egypt, the seas, the city of Dumah, the desert plains, the "valley of vision," and the region of Tyre. Throughout this section, a common theme continues: Trust in God, not idols or human empires.

As Assyria, the dominant empire in the region, threatens Judah from the north, many in Judah sought a military alliance with Egypt. But Isaiah warns that protection comes through trusting in God alone, not through making alliances with other countries. He foretells of civil war in Egypt and of its ultimate fall to the Assyrians. Yet Isaiah also offers a vision of a time of peace between Egypt, Judah, and Assyria, when all will worship the God of Israel.

Trailblazers

- Isaiah
- Egyptians
- People of Sidon and Tyre
- King Sargon and the Assyrians
- Shebna
- Eliakim

• What could be a more faithful attitude for the Israelites?

WEEK
1
◆
DAY
5

• How would our society be different were we to fully trust in God's power? How would your life be different?

Racing Tip

Isaiah 21:1-10 claims to address the wilderness of the sea, then talks about camels and kingdoms of the land, and refers to the fall of Babylon. If you're confused, you're not alone. This section has long baffled scholars, who have come to very different conclusions about its meaning.

2 NOW READ ISAIAH 19–23.

3 Switchback

In previous legs, we read that God calls Abraham to leave his home for a new place, Moses to stand up to Pharaoh, and Deborah to lead an army in a male-dominated society. God instructs Isaiah, however, to walk around naked for three years—apparently as a warning not to trust in an alliance with Egypt, whose people will be led away naked as prisoners by the Assyrians.

The greater meaning to the symbol of nakedness to show how exposed and unprotected Israel and Judah are without God. (The Hebrew word for *naked* means "vulnerable" as well as "nude.") We, too, are exposed and unprotected without God. Just as the Israelites thought the Egyptians covered them, we trust in things other than God to protect us.

• What are the "Egypts," things you trust in other than God, in your life?

• What have been the consequences of trusting in these things?

Road Signs

• **Ashdod:** This Philistine city near the Mediterranean coast fell during the Assyrian invasion.
• **Tyre:** This major port city in Lebanon, north of Israel, was originally partly on the mainland and partly on an island. Tyre had close relations with Israel during the reigns of David and Solomon.
• **"Ships of Tarshish":** Tarshish, another major port city in the Mediterranean, was known for its trade with Tyre. (In the Book of Jonah [1:3; 4:2], Jonah attempts to run away from God's call, taking a ship bound for Tarshish.)

4 Prayer

God of the naked and the exposed, remove the broken armor of the world that covers us. Instead, clothe us in your grace, love, and commitment to us. Amen.

Water Break

Well done! You've made it through the first week of reading Isaiah, a book full of short chapters but with some confusing ideas to grasp. Press on to Week 2!

A Prayer to God
Isaiah 24–27

① Scouting the Terrain

Prayers make up much of this section of Isaiah, including visions of the kind of future for which the prophet is praying. In prayers we offer thanks for all God has done in our lives. We also pray for what we hope God will do.

Trailblazer

• Isaiah

As you read these prayers, remember that Isaiah is a prophet to a hurting people. By this point in the Book of Isaiah, the Assyrians have conquered the northern kingdom of Israel and are threatening the southern kingdom of Judah. In addition to political insecurity, many of the people to whom Isaiah was speaking were poor. Prayers like these gave the people hope by reminding them of what God had promised to do in the days to come.

• How can a vision of something that seems far off help sustain people through hard times to come?

• What promises has God made to you?

• How do these promises apply to something going on in your life now?

Pace Pusher

Try reading it out loud:
• 25:7-10a
• 26:8-9a

② NOW READ ISAIAH 24–27.

③ Switchback

We have already seen how sweeping God's concern was. God did not just address Israel and Judah but also the surrounding kingdoms. Chapter 24 suggests a reason for this universal concern that goes beyond God's universal power.

Everything is connected. The world has been woven together in such a way that what affects one affects all. Evils and injustices committed by a few people cause whole societies, even the whole earth, to languish and suffer. Isaiah says that God is looking for a radical change in the people of Israel and Judah—a recommitment to God's justice and righteousness. And through that commitment, the world will see what God desires for all humankind.

• How have the actions of others had a negative effect on you?

• How can acts of kindness and service have a positive impact on people other than the recipients of these acts?

Racing Tip

The following lines from Isaiah 25:8-9 have been rewritten so that they address the reader, using the words *I, me,* and *my.* Read them aloud several times.

Then the Lord GOD will wipe away the tears from my face and will take away my disgrace from the earth, for the LORD has spoken. I will say on that day:

"This is my God; I have waited for God to save me. This is the LORD for whom I have waited; I will be glad and rejoice in God's salvation."

Do you think that God speaks these words to you as they were spoken through Isaiah 2,500 years ago?

 ④ Prayer

Steadfast God, remind us that our actions affect people far and wide. Teach us to live healthy lives and so nurture the body of Christ.

Process and Product
Isaiah 28–31

1 Scouting the Terrain

In Isaiah's time, Assyria is the region's most powerful nation. The people of Judah, like their neighbors, fear that the Assyrians will conquer them. For security, the Judahite leaders seek an ally in another powerful nation, Egypt, hoping that, together, they can defeat the Assyrians. It sounds like a good plan; it makes sense. Egypt has thousands of horses and chariots. From a human perspective, Egypt seems to be Judah's only realistic hope.

Trailblazers
- **Isaiah**
- **Egypt**

Chapters 30–31 focus on God's reaction to the plan to enlist the Egyptians. The prophet announces that the alliance will bring disaster. Why? The people are looking for protection from human kingdoms, instead of turning to God. It's not that other nations have no roles to play in helping Judah. Instead, those roles must be appointed by God. By running to Egypt, the people have cut God out of the process.

• When have you failed to include God in your decision-making?

• How can you involve God more in your decision-making?

2 NOW READ ISAIAH 28–31.

3 Switchback

God is doing an awful lot of work in the world—bringing down kingdoms, inspiring wars, and teaching lessons. Surely Isaiah was asked (or asked himself):"Why?" Why must God's chosen people endure so much pain? Isn't there an easier way?

To answer the question, Isaiah reminds his audience how food is made. Grain must be ground or beaten to produce something useful. If God is to truly use Israel and Judah as chosen people for the world, they must be refined. In the midst of the analogy, however, Isaiah notices that grain may be beaten but not pulverized, crushed into flour but not trampled on forever. There is an end to the suffering; and through the suffering, God will create something great.

Road Sign

• **Ariel:** This was an altar hearth or a place to burn an offering.

• How has God used hard times in your life to make you a better Christian?

4 Prayer

God, help the suffering to pass. Refine us so that you can use us for the good of your world. Amen.

The Dangers of Complacency
Isaiah 32–35

1 Scouting the Terrain

We have seen oracles that identify such sins as arrogance, forgetting God, and cruelty. Isaiah 32:9-12 calls a new group of people—the complacent—to repent. To Isaiah, those who are complacent or "at ease" commit the sin of self-centeredness. They're rich and happy, embodying the attitude of "I've got mine; you get yours." Because they show no concern for the poor or for injustice and unrighteousness in their society, they violate the inseparable commandments to love God and to love their neighbors.

Isaiah calls on them to wear sackcloth (think burlap) as an act of repentance; putting on uncomfortable clothing was meant to remind people that they were to be uncomfortable with their own sin.

• Can you think of an example of suffering about which many people in our world have remained complacent? What can you do to address this suffering?

Trailblazers

• God
• Isaiah
• Judah
• Edom

2 NOW READ ISAIAH 32–35.

3 Switchback

God's judgment has a profound effect on the entire region. People suffer when their crops fail, homes and cities become ruins, farms and vineyards become overgrown with thorns and briars. Wild animals—ostriches, jackals, hyenas and wildcats—replace the cattle, sheep, and goats that people had raised. The land turns to sulfur, making it infertile; and streams are clogged with pitch (tar). Think about the post-apocalyptic visions of deserted cities you may have seen in movies. All of these, Isaiah suggests, are the effects of unrighteousness.

In contrast, chapters 35 and 32:15-20 offer a vision of what happens when God's spirit is poured out on the land. Streams will flow in the desert. Barren places will bloom. The blind, deaf and mute will be healed. All creation will be transformed. God's kingdom of justice and righteousness will prevail, and the effects of righteousness will be peace, quietness and trust (32:17).

• In what ways does the whole land reap the consequence of human sin (or human righteousness) today?

fast forward Research the life of a medieval monk or Christian mystic, such as Protestant reformer Martin Luther or nun Teresa of Avila, who practiced rituals of self-mortification to test his or her faith. For an entire day, wear uncomfortable clothing: a shirt that's too small around the neck or arms, a scratchy sweater, winter clothes on a hot day, shoes that pinch. Each time you feel discomfort, think about your sins and ways that you haven't cared about the needs of others. Then compare and contrast your experience with the results of your research. What is beneficial to your Christian journey about the practice? What, if anything, is detrimental to your faith?

Record your thoughts throughout the day on a video diary or on your race blog, which must be an genuine expression of your day's events and what you learned from the experience. Upload your video on *amazingbiblerace.com* or show your blog post(s) to your team leader for points.

4 Prayer

God, forgive us for our complacency. Help us identify the ways in which we need to do your work, and help us follow through with that work. Amen.

Oh, No You Didn't, Assyria!
Isaiah 36–40

1 Scouting the Terrain

After 36 chapters of near non-stop oracles and addresses, almost all in verse form, we finally get a story with a plot. Chapters 36–39 tell of Assyria's invasion of Judah in 701 B.C. (a couple decades after Assyria's destruction of the Northern Kingdom of Israel).

Hezekiah, the king of Judah and a descendant of David, has good reason to fear. Assyria's army is much larger and more technologically advanced than Judah's. After capturing the fortified towns of Judah, the Assyrians encircle and besiege Jerusalem. Speaking to the people in their own language, Rabshakeh, a messenger of King Sennacherib of Assyria, warns what will happen if the city does not surrender. He also mocks God. In response, Isaiah prophesies against Sennacherib's arrogance and reassures Hezekiah that God will defend them.

Trailblazers

- Hezekiah
- Sennacherib
- Rabshakeh
- Eliakim
- Shebna
- Joah
- Merodach-baladan

WEEK 2 ◇ DAY 4

• What behavior have you seen that you would describe as "mocking God"? Explain.

• When have you ever seen or faced a situation that looked so hopeless that it was hard to trust in God?

Pace Pusher

Try reading aloud:
- 40:10-11
- 40:28-31

2 NOW READ ISAIAH 36–40.

3 Switchback

You may have noticed a big shift between chapters 39 and 40. That's because the story jumps ahead by 150 years. Bible scholars believe that these later chapters were written by a different prophet, whom scholars often call "Second Isaiah," who followed in the tradition of the original Isaiah.

When Chapter 39 ends, the Assyrian invasion has been repelled, but destruction at the hands of the Babylonians is still on the way. As Chapter 40 begins, the people of Judah have been in exile in Babylon for decades. Jerusalem has been destroyed, and the Temple lies in ruins. But they have now paid the penalty for their sins. God is ready to bring them home. In fact, God is building a road from Babylon across the impassable desert. It's not a literal highway but is Isaiah's vision that God is still in charge of events and will restore Jerusalem and its people.

• Where in your experience has God "made a highway through the desert," providing a solution to a seemingly impossible situation?

• What does it mean to "wait on the LORD"?

 Imagine that you are in exile in Babylon and have somehow heard of Isaiah's words in Chapter 40. Write a letter to a relative back in Judah and tell him or her why your hope in God has been renewed. Research writing practices in Babylon around 700 B.C., including the type of paper, ink, and seals used. As closely as possible, recreate your letter using authentic materials (you may use today's English language). Then scan or photograph your letter and upload it to *amazingbiblerace.com* for points.

 Prayer

Everlasting God, although we grow faint and weary, give us the faith to wait on you to see us through. Amen

Tuning In
to 'Babylonian Idol'
Isaiah 41–44

1. Scouting the Terrain

As God's soliloquy continues, we get a clue about how hard things are for the people of Judah. They have been conquered by the Babylonians. The people have scattered and no are longer connected to one another (see 43:5-7). Ostriches and jackals live in their land (43:20)—a sign that the land is no longer "clean."

Trailblazers

- God
- Isaiah
- Israel

One of the greatest threats facing God's chosen people is the prevalence of idols among the Babylonians. God issues a stern warning against idols: Nothing can be greater than its maker. Isaiah makes a persuasive argument (44:9-20) for why idols have no power; all that they have has been given to them by their human makers. How could human-made idols have power over human beings? God's power comes from the fact that God made us, knows us intimately, and has love for us that goes beyond the love of a mother for her baby.

• In what ways do people still rely on false gods or idols?

Isaiah 42:1-17 speaks of salvation for Israel through God's servant. Use a concordance or a study Bible to see where key terms in Isaiah appear in the New Testament. Some terms you may want to focus on: *chosen one, Spirit, justice, light, free, lead the blind.* Who is God's servant? How is Israel ultimately saved? Take a quiz at *amazingbiblerace.com* to see how much you've learned.

2. NOW READ ISAIAH 41–44.

3 Switchback

These chapters contain powerful imagery: a distraught God who is hurt by Israel's offenses; a God who deeply desires to care for and be loved by God's people; and a God who must be just and true to God's self. Maybe it helps us imagine just how much God must have endured with the unfaithfulness of Israel and Judah.

• What "fires" are you walking through in your life? How have you felt God's presence during these times?

Road Signs

• **Threshing sledge:** This farm implement was used to cut grass or wheat.
• **Jeshurun** (JESH-uh-ruhn)**:** This was God's term of endearment for Israel, meaning "dearest upright one."

4 Prayer

Spend some time in silence and then pray this prayer adapted from Isaiah 43. Don't rush; let the words sink in.

I will not fear, for you have redeemed me. You have called me by name. I am yours. When I pass through the waters, you will be with me; and the rivers will not overwhelm me. When I walk through fire, I shall not be burned and the flame shall not consume me. For you are the Lord my God, the Holy One of Israel. I am precious in your sight and honored. You love me. I will not fear, for you are with me. Amen.

Water Break

You've made it through two-thirds of the longest prophetic book of the Bible. But don't be in a hurry. Remember, Jesus quoted Isaiah more than any other book, except Psalms. Savor these rich messages of God's enduring faithfulness as sustenance for the rest of your journey.

The Vengeance of God
Isaiah 45–48

 Scouting the Terrain

Isaiah 45–48 is God's address to the Babylonians, who have enjoyed 70 years of rule over the Israelites. Now God is bringing their dominance to an end. Israel has paid the price for its sin. So God informs the Babylonians that Cyrus, king of Persia (current-day Iran), will crush Babylon. Cyrus is God's instrument. God is in control.

Trailblazer

• **King Cyrus**

By telling the Babylonians, in a mocking tone, "Remove your veil, strip off your robe, [and] uncover your legs" (47:2), Isaiah reminds them that they are vulnerable and impure. (The veil is a symbol of purity.) God tells the Babylonians to seek help from their astrologers, knowing that astrologers have no power. In Chapter 48, God makes sure that the Babylonians understand that they defeated God's people only because God allowed it to happen.

• God can use anyone, even conquering rulers. Whom has God used in your own life to help you walk more closely with God?

2. **NOW READ ISAIAH 45–48.**

③ Switchback

When God sends Cyrus against Babylon, it is not just to end the pain of God's people. It's also as an act of judgment against Babylon. God allowed the Babylonians to take control of Judah, but they squandered their authority. As God tells them: "You said, 'I shall be mistress forever,' so that you did not lay these things to heart or remember their end' " (47:7). The rest of Chapter 47 makes it obvious that the Babylonians have not trusted in God. Instead, they've relied on sorcery, astrology, and cruelty. Babylon missed a chance to connect with God and receive mercy rather than wrath.

• When have you missed opportunities to connect with God?

> ### Road Sign
>
> • **Bel and Nebo:** These were gods in Babylonian mythology. Bel, another name for the God Marduk, was the chief of the gods. Nebo was his son.

• Throughout Isaiah, God uses unlikely people to do God's work. When have you seen God work through someone you wouldn't have expected? What happened?

④ Prayer

God, help us see you at work in unlikely people and in unlikely places. Grant us eyes to see opportunities to hold close to you. Amen.

Suffering Servant
Isaiah 49–53

1 Scouting the Terrain

Today you'll read the first references in the Bible to a mysterious character who is usually referred to as the "suffering servant." Early Christians read these passages and saw them as prophecies that predicted Jesus' death and resurrection. There are striking similarities between Jesus and the suffering servant. Both are teachers who endure pain and humiliation (50:4-9). Both were despised, hurt for the sins of others. Neither resorted to violence (53:1-12). Look for these and other similarities as you read.

Trailblazers

• **Suffering Servant**

But it is also important to look at these passages as Isaiah's original audience would have seen them. These words had deep meaning to those who were suffering— perhaps suffering for the good of others. To the exiles of Judah, the servant represents their own people, who have suffered double the punishment for their sin (40:2). Why? Perhaps they suffered so that others would learn something about God or to give God reason to remove the Babylonians from power. They were coming to understand that God "chose" them as a special people not just to be rewarded but to be servants who would bring the understanding of the one true God to all humankind.

• In addition to those above, what ideas do you have about who and/or what the "suffering servant" represents? Go online to share your thoughts and read the ideas of other runners in the Amazing Bible Race.

2 NOW READ ISAIAH 49–53.

3 Switchback

"See, I have inscribed you on the palms of my hands." (Isaiah 49:16). What do you write on your hands? A phone number? An e-mail address? Maybe you write down a website you want to check out or your homework assignment. Your hand is a good place to write a reminder; after all, you see your hands all the time.

It's a powerful notion to think that our names are inscribed on God's hands. Don't get hung up on an image of God physically writing on actual hands with an actual pen. Think of it this way: Instead of being merely written on God's hands, as with ink that fades, we are inscribed—etched into the surface.

• Can you explain how God is always with us, yet there are still places in our lives we need to let God enter?

4 Prayer

God we thank you for the way you always remember us. Help us always think of you as we run the race of life. Amen.

The Extra Mile

Write "God" on your hand with a permanent marker. See if whether makes a difference in your life over the next couple days. When you are reminded of God on a more regular basis, do you act differently? Do other people respond to you differently when they see *God* written on your hand?

Read Isaiah 53 and the account of Christ's crucifixion from Mark 15:16-41. Discuss with your team how Christ fulfills the role of Isaiah's "suffering servant."

Before completing the quiz for points at *amazingbiblerace.com*, meditate on Christ's suffering on your behalf and record your thoughts in your blog.

Isaiah, the Sports Reporter
Isaiah 54–58

1 Scouting the Terrain

Trailblazer

• Isaiah

Imagine a two-person race. On the radio, an announcer gives play-by-play commentary, going back and forth between the two athletes: "Smith pulls ahead. Jones adjusts her form and widens her stride. Now Smith is really sweating!"

In Isaiah 56:9–57:21, the author uses a similar technique to show the contrast between the results of righteousness and the results of wickedness. Remember that his audience was used to hearing God's word proclaimed aloud. The speaker may have used tone of voice or hand gestures to help the audience keep track. To aid your understanding of this section, use highlighters to mark which sections refer to the wicked and which to the righteous. Also, you may notice some differences in language and style starting in Isaiah 56. Many scholars believe that chapters 56–66 were written by a different author after the exiles had returned from Babylon. They call this author "Third Isaiah."

• What are some differences between hearing God's Word read aloud and reading God's Word to yourself? Which do you prefer? Why?

fast forward

When promising comfort to Judah, God offers food. Food is one of the greatest ways that one person can show love for another. Cook dinner for your family or friends, spoon-feed your baby sibling, or get lunch for a person who is homeless and eat with him or her. Make a video diary of the experience (with the other person's permission) in which you answer these questions:

• How does feeding someone change the way you feel or think about that person?
• How did this person respond when you offered to feed him or her? Why, do you think, did he or she respond in that way?

Upload your video to *amazingbiblerace.com* for points.

3 Switchback

This is one of the most frightening lines in Scripture: "For a brief moment I abandoned you" (54:7). What? It's frightening to think that God could abandon us. Why did God do it? God was angry. But God's anger could also be reassuring. We get angry only about things and people that matter. That God cared enough to be angry reveals the depth of God's love and compassion.

Compassion (see 54:8) means "to suffer with." When Judah suffered, so did God. The pain of Judah's sin was so great that God had to step away. But there is good news: "The mountains may depart, and the hills may be removed, but my steadfast love shall not depart from you, says the Lord, who has compassion on you" (Isaiah 54:10).

2 NOW READ ISAIAH 54–58.

Road Sign

• **Sentinels:** The sentinels Isaiah speaks of were prophets or other leaders who claimed to interpret God's message.

• It's important to remember that anger does not always equal love. What are some examples of where this is the case?

• When has your anger been an expression of love?

4 Prayer

God, you will not leave or forsake us. We can always count on you. Thank you for caring so much, for sharing in our pain and running the race of life with us. Amen.

The Bystander Effect
Isaiah 59–62

1) Scouting the Terrain

Trailblazer
• Isaiah

In 1964 a woman named Kitty Genovese was stabbed to death near her New York home. The murder took about thirty minutes and was witnessed by dozens of people, none of whom tried to stop the attack. The Kitty Genovese case is probably the most famous of several stories in which bystanders failed to help a victim. Social psychologists who have studied this phenomenon have found that people are significantly less likely to help in a crisis if other people are around. Why? They assume that someone among the crowd is more qualified to respond than they are.

The reality is that we all let injustice occur. We know, for example, that if we send more money to a world hunger charity, fewer children will die of starvation. But, like those who witnessed Kitty Genovese's murder, we may assume that, if we don't help, someone else will. When more people think this way, more people die of starvation.

• God saw injustice and was appalled (59:15-16). How could the children of the God of justice let this happen?

• How do we continue to let injustice happen today?

Pace Pusher

Read it aloud:
• 60:1-3
• 62:10

2) NOW READ ISAIAH 59–62.

3 Switchback

Rub some olive oil (or other cooking oil) between your fingers. Pay attention to what it feels like. Are your hands softer than they were before? Isaiah 61:3 refers to "the oil of gladness." Oil is a symbol of God's attitude toward the people. Oil coats and spreads whatever it touches. It stays with us (your hands probably still smell like olive oil). It's hard to wash off.

When God wants to give the people "the oil of gladness instead of mourning," God wants them to be coated in a joy that is not easily washed away. God wants persistent joy for the people.

• What would it take for you to live as though you were coated with an "oil of gladness"?

Road Sign

• **"Suck the milk of nations"** (60:16): This is a poetic way of saying that God's people will benefit from the wealth of neighboring countries.

4 Prayer

God of joy, help us be coated with your gladness. Amen.

It's not Always Easy
Isaiah 63—66

1 **Scouting the Terrain**

Our relationship with God is frequently difficult. The people of Judah have gone through tremendous grief and pain. They cry out to

God, struggle with God and ask hard questions. Since God is all-powerful, they wonder whether God caused them to rebel. Did God want their sin and punishment to happen? "Why, O Lord, do you make us stray from your ways and harden our hearts, so that we do not fear you?" (63:17a). They also wonder whether God is still listening: "There is no one who calls on your name, or attempts to take hold of you; for you have hidden your face from us" (64:7).

Deep down, these questions force us to examine how we understand God.

• Did God want the people to suffer? If so, why?

• Did God hide from the Israelites? Would God hide from us?

• Do we have a right to question what God does in the world? Why, or why not?

2 **NOW READ ISAIAH 63—66.**

③ Switchback

Isaiah covers a lot of ground, spanning generations, kingdoms, and cultures. Judah and other nations are judged. God's chosen endure exile in Babylon. The Temple lies in ruins. It looks like the end of Israel. After 70 years, though, God raises up Cyrus, the Persian king, against Babylon. Some exiles return home. God promises that the people will live in security and peace. "For as the new heavens and the new earth, which I will make, shall remain before me, says the LORD, so shall your descendants and your name remain" (66:22). God renews the covenant to be the God of Israel forever.

Road Sign

• **Fortune** and **Destiny** (65:11): These are names for pagan gods.

• Reread Isaiah 65. What blessings does God have in store for the faithful?

• Why does God, who is merciful, punish the wicked?

Water Break

You've made it through Isaiah, the longest of the prophetic books! It can be a hard one to read because it describes so much of God's anger. Now take a break. You'll need your rest to get through Jeremiah!

④ Prayer

God, thank you for keeping your eye upon us. Thank you for remaining faithful to us even when we are not faithful to you. In this long race, thank you for remaining strong even as our legs give out. Amen.

The Nature of Prophecy
Jeremiah 1–4

1 Scouting the Terrain

In calling Jeremiah, God instructs him to "gird up your loins" (1:17)—or, as we might put it today, "roll up your sleeves." In those days, men

Trailblazers
• **God**
• **Jeremiah**

prepared for battle or strenuous work by pulling up the back hem of their robe or tunic up between their legs (loins) and tucking it into their belt in the front so that their clothing wouldn't get in the way. God was telling Jeremiah to get ready for a struggle; because telling people that they're doing wrong and will have to pay the consequences generally doesn't make a person very popular. But that's what prophets do.

• Who are the prophets in your community or in our world today? In other words, who are the people who hold us accountable for our actions and challenge us to be more faithful to God's will?

The Extra Mile

Have you ever wondered whether God has emotions? Some tend to think of God as immovable and passionless. In verses 2:5-12, however, God sounds hurt and used. This pain turns to anger and then once again to sadness. Pay attention to God's emotions as you reread this section.

2 NOW READ JEREMIAH 1–4.

③ Switchback

You heard right: God called Israel a "whore." It's not a word you'd usually hear in church. Are you shocked? Good! Expressions like this, in their proper context, are powerful and show real emotion in a way that polite language might not. When Jeremiah uses a word like *whore,* it is supposed to offend, shock, and teach us about how hurt God was by Judah's unfaithfulness.

• How have you been unfaithful to God? What can you do to return to God?

• What "great things" might God be calling you to do with your life?

• What excuses do you make to keep from doing these "great things"?

Jeremiah 1 tells about Jeremiah's call to be God's prophet. Study the calls of Isaiah (Isaiah 6:1-13) and Ezekiel (Ezekiel 2:1–3:11). Note how God's calls to these men are similar and how they are different. Consider these questions as you study:

• What is each man's response to God's call?
• What is God's answer to the response?
• What happens to each prophet's mouth?
• Why is the mouth significant in the prophet's call?
• How is God described?

Discuss your answers with your team. After your discussion, take a quiz on *amazingbiblerace.com* to earn points.

Road Sign

• **"Committing adultery with stone and tree"** (3:9): This is a way to say that people are committing idolatry by worshiping gods made of stone and wood.

④ Prayer

God, thank you for your constant presence. Remind me that you will always equip me to carry out your will. Amen.

Healing Carelessly
Jeremiah 5–9

① Scouting the Terrain

Parts of Jeremiah read like laundry lists of things that God's people have done wrong. Surely, though, the people have done something right, right? Chapters 5–9 don't seem to suggest that they have. God challenges Jeremiah to find just one righteous person so that God would have an excuse not to destroy Jerusalem. God says, "They have treated the wound of my people carelessly, saying 'Peace, peace,' when there is no peace" (6:14; 8:11). Then God adds, "We look for peace, but find no good" (8:15; 14:19). In other words, they not only have ignored the most vulnerable people in their society, but they also have lied about the true state of affairs, claiming that things are fine when they are not.

Trailblazers

• **God**
• **Jeremiah**

Our culture is sometimes guilty of healing carelessly. For example, some of us believe that the civil rights movement ended segregation and racial discrimination in schools and businesses. Some of us think that, by giving a few dollars, we've done our part to end poverty. Jeremiah is here to tell us otherwise.

• What are other issues that people in our culture think are resolved but are actually healed only lightly?

• What situations in your life have you "healed lightly"?

② NOW READ JEREMIAH 5–9.

3 Switchback

Do any of these verses sound familiar? Have you ever described anyone the way Jeremiah describes God's people in 9:8? To the list of awful sins they have committed, the prophet adds (paraphrasing): "They don't say very nice things about one another, and they do mean stuff behind one another's back."

Jeremiah reminds us that our words can hurt *and* that our words matter to God. If you have been wounded by the words of others, do not think that God ignores your pain. God knows your pain and will always be with you. God also wants you to be aware of the pain that you, with your own words, inflict on others.

• When has your tongue become "a deadly arrow"? How has what you've said hurt your friends and peers?

• When have you spoken friendly words to someone even though you didn't really mean them?

 Heal something "heavily." It could be a relationship with a friend whom you have previously ignored or healed only lightly. It could be a campaign your team launches at your school to address an important issue. The team should choose at least one "healing." This could be a group effort or something an individual chooses. Keep a journal or a video diary documenting your experience. Then upload your work at *amazingbiblerace.com* for points.

 Prayer

God of peace, comfort us with the knowledge that you have felt it all, seen it all, heard it all, and know it all. We are not alone.
Thank you. Amen.

A Hurt God
Jeremiah 10–14

 Scouting the Terrain

WEEK

4
◆
DAY

3

Trailblazers
• **God**
• **Jeremiah**

Have you ever been really hurt by someone you trusted? Think about how you felt. Now multiply the intensity of those feelings by infinity. That's how God strongly felt about the people of Judah.

In Jeremiah 10–14, we get several glimpses into God's pain, suffering, and anger. In Chapter 11, God expresses an inability to trust the serially unfaithful people of Judah. By the end of Chapter 13, God is enraged. This is the kind of pain that comes only from someone who has been betrayed by the one he or she loves. Is there anything comforting in this section? Read and see.

• What is frightening about the anger of God? What is comforting or even hopeful?

• Why do loving parents sometimes become angry with their children? How do we know that a parent or grandparent still loves us even when he or she is angry with us?

2 **NOW READ JEREMIAH 10–14.**

③ Switchback

In 12:1, Jeremiah argues with God. (You might even say that Jeremiah brings charges against God.) Jeremiah knows that he will lose, because he knows that God is infinite in wisdom and power. Still, Jeremiah is overcome by the pain in the world and wonders why people who do evil continue to prosper.

Many of us sometimes have questions about God or have trouble making sense of what God is doing. These questions and struggles are OK. Even Jeremiah, who spoke for God, had questions. Don't be afraid to go to God with tough questions or even complaints. Even if you know that God is right, there is a value to the argument and the discussion.

• What challenging questions do you have for God?

Reread verse 10:11. God tells Jeremiah to tell the people about other gods that will perish. What other gods is God talking about? What are some of the other "gods" that we worship in our culture today? For more help, take an online quiz at *amazingbiblerace.com*.

Prayer

God, even though your wisdom is infinite, we sometimes need to struggle with your wisdom because ours is less than infinite. Thank you for meeting us where we are, accepting our struggles, and accepting us. Amen.

Training
Jeremiah 15–19

 Scouting the Terrain

If you've been going to church for a while, you've probably experienced an object lesson. An object lesson uses a common item to make a point or convey an important truth. Object lessons usually involve metaphors. For example, an apple and a seed might be used to teach a lesson on how God can take the gifts that we've been given and make them grow and bear fruit.

Trailblazers
• God
• Jeremiah

God uses a lot of object lessons to teach Jeremiah. In Chapter 18, God sends Jeremiah down to the potter's house to show the prophet how God will reshape and restore God's people. In Chapter 13, God uses a dirty loincloth—rigid, stiff, stained shorts—to show how useless and unclean Israel has become to God. These vivid demonstrations help us remember the truth that God reveals through the prophet.

• What important lessons have you learned through an experience or illustration, rather than by words alone?

WEEK
4

DAY
4

 Find a local potter and conduct an interview with him or her. Ask some of the following questions as well as some of your own. You might even choose to have the potter react to Jeremiah 18:1-11. If possible, while you're there, make a pot yourself.

• How gentle or rough do you need to be as you work with the clay?
• Have you ever gotten frustrated when working with clay? What led to your frustration?
• How do you know when to start over with clay that you have worked really hard on but that did not come out the way you had intended?

Post a video of your interview and pottery experience at *amazingbiblerace.com* for points. (Be sure to get permission from the potter before you even begin taping.) If you were able to make a piece of pottery, upload photos or video of your creation as well.

3 Switchback

In 14:13-16, we learned of other prophets who said that God had revealed to them the opposite of what God had revealed to Jeremiah. According to these other prophets, God's message for Judah was: "You shall not see the sword, nor shall you have famine, but I will give you true peace in this place."

Jeremiah, though he is the true prophet, has the burden of speaking God's true, but very unpopular, message. Given two conflicting sources of information, people tend to believe what they want to hear. We like news that reinforces our existing beliefs, and we listen to people with whom we agree. Often, however, God wants to tell us things that we don't want to hear.

• When have you ignored a message simply because you did not like it? What happened as a result?

2 NOW READ JEREMIAH 15–19.

• How can we tell who truly speaks for God and who merely claims to speak for God?

4 Prayer

Master Potter, rework our imperfections, refine us with your skilled hands, and make us as you want us to be. Amen.

Homeland Security
Jeremiah 20–23

 Scouting the Terrain

In biblical times land represented life and independence. Anyone who did not own land had to rely on others for food. These people would sometimes sell themselves into slavery to someone with a lot of land so that they would be assured of food to eat and a place to live.

Land also represented God's promises to God's people. For the people of Judah, their land was the fulfillment of God's covenant with them. Going into exile in Babylon was much more than being forced to move to a neighboring country. The exile separated the people from their most sacred connection to God.

Trailblazers

• God
• Jeremiah
• Pashhur
• Zephaniah
• King Zedekiah
• King Nebuchadrezzar
• King Jehoiakim
• King Jehoiachin

• What value does our society place on owning land?

• What would be the most difficult thing about moving to a foreign country, with a different language and culture?

NOW READ JEREMIAH 20–23.

③ Switchback

Jeremiah has a tough job. He has to proclaim an unpopular message of doom and destruction to his own people. Not surprisingly, he suffers for his work. Chapter 20 begins with Jeremiah being put into the stocks (an uncomfortable form of public humiliation and punishment) and ends with one of the saddest prayers of suffering ever written. In Chapter 1 God appointed Jeremiah "a prophet to the nations" (1:5). Now we see the depth of suffering that comes with such a calling.

• What unpopular messages do today's church leaders proclaim?

• Whom do you know of from history or nowadays who has suffered for speaking an unpopular truth?

• If you live an outspoken life for Christ, what unpleasant things might you have to endure?

④ Prayer

God of life and land, root us in your kingdom and give us the strength and courage to proclaim to the world the message of your kingdom. Amen.

Water Break

You have now completed Week 4 of Leg 4. Well done! But get ready: You and Jeremiah have two more weeks of suffering for God to look forward to.

Finally ... Hope!
Jeremiah 24–26

 Scouting the Terrain

Jeremiah takes a sharp turn this week. After 23 chapters promising destruction, we finally begin to see signs of hope for Israel. But it comes only after the dire promise has been fulfilled. In Chapter 24 we flash-forward to when the Babylonians, under the rule of King Nebuchadrezzar, have invaded Judah, captured its rulers and sent them to Babylon, just as Jeremiah had prophesied.

Trailblazers

• **God**
• **Jeremiah**
• **King Jehoiakim**
• **King Nebuchadrezzar**
• **Various unfaithful priests and prophets**

Then God reveals new plans. There's good news—although not for everyone. In this little glimpse of the future, Jeremiah says that some people will safely return, by God's hand, to Jerusalem; while others are doomed to exile and shame. As you read this week, stay on the lookout for those who can look forward to comfort and those who are promised further distress.

• Why would God made different promises to different groups?

**NOW READ
JEREMIAH 24–26.**

Switchback

Jeremiah 26 gives us a glimpse of just how dangerous it is to be a prophet. People are sick of hearing Jeremiah's message of destruction. They seek to silence him permanently. Jeremiah responds to such threats with incredible courage. He challenges them to "do with me as seems good and right to you" (26:14), cleverly reminding them that they alone will be held accountable for what they are about to do. Then he reveals what will happen to them if they kill him.

Although Jeremiah is spared, the risks of being a prophet are always high. We are told of other prophets that preached a similar message and were hunted down and killed.

- Why, do you think, were prophets often so disliked that people wanted to kill them?

Road Sign

- **Seventy years** (25:11): In the Hebrew tradition, seven was a number of wholeness or completeness. Seventy years suggests that the sin of the people is so great that it will take that long to reestablish the relationship between God and God's people. It also suggests that the exiles will die in a foreign land. The hope of a return to Judah is for their children and grandchildren.

 ## Prayer

God, we ask that you would help us identify the true prophets of our time. Give us the courage of Jeremiah to stand up for you. Amen.

One Last Try
Jeremiah 27–29

① Scouting the Terrain

When you were a child, did your parents ever put you in "time out"? The exile in Babylon was like a long time out. God makes the people live for 70 years in Babylon and then "when you call upon me and come and pray to me, I will hear you" (29:12). God hasn't abandoned the covenant relationship. God has just put the responsibility for that relationship squarely upon the people. Just as your parents probably said to you, God was saying, "Let me know when you're ready to behave."

We know that God is always present and is eagerly waiting for us. But sometimes we think that God is hard to find. Maybe it's because we aren't really looking or aren't ready to live God's way. Through Jeremiah, God tells the exiles, "When you search for me, you will find me; if you seek me with all your heart, I will let you find me" (29:13).

• When does God seem hard for you to find?

Trailblazers

• **God**
• **Jeremiah**
• **King Zedekiah of Judah**
• **Various kings of neighboring countries**
• **King Jeconiah**
• **Prophet Hananiah**
• **Priest Zephaniah**
• **King Nebuchadnezzar**
• **King Nebuchadrezzar**

• Where does the responsibility lie with our relationship with God? How does God reach out to us? In what ways must we reach out to God?

② NOW READ JEREMIAH 27–29.

3 Switchback

Throughout the books of the prophets, we find oracles announcing the doom of Israel's enemies. But here Jeremiah throws us a curve ball. Not only does he instruct the people not to resist the Babylonians, he urges them to pray for their well-being. Put down roots. Marry and multiply.

The reason seems simple at first. The well-being of the exiles will be tied to that of the Babylonians. But there's more to it than that. In Jeremiah, we see hints of Jesus' message not to violently resist the political authorities; if a Roman soldier makes you carry his pack for one mile, Jesus told his followers, go a second mile as well (Matthew 5:41). Why not fight those who would conquer us? Jeremiah (and Jesus) teach that we don't need to worry about being in control of events. That's God's job. Our job is to love God and neighbor.

- How might working for the good of the conquering Babylonians have been a radical expression of faith in God?

- Which authority figures do you most have trouble obeying? Why?

Road Sign

- **Yoke** (27:2): This was a frame used by two oxen to pull heavy loads. A yoke was often used as a symbol of servitude or hardship.

4 Prayer

Ever-present God, you can be our hiding place from the pain of the world; yet sometimes we have a hard time finding you. Help us learn to seek you with our whole heart. Amen.

Jeremiah

Remembering the Past and Moving Forward
Jeremiah 30–31

1 Scouting the Terrain

Jeremiah reminds the people of just how ancient is the connection between God and Israel. It goes back before there even was "Israel." Remember how, in Genesis, God gave Jacob a new name, Israel, that means "he who wrestles with God" (Genesis 32:24-32)? Like its patriarch Jacob did, the whole nation of Israel is wrestling with God.

By calling upon the beginnings of Israel, God is calling Israel to a new beginning. God proclaims, "O virgin Israel!" (31:4), signifying that Israel is being given a fresh start and hope for the future.

• Reread Genesis 32:24-32. How might knowing that Jacob wrestled with God (and that the struggle ended with a blessing) have been comforting for the exiles?

Trailblazers

• God
• Jeremiah
• Israel
• Judah

• When has hope come out of a seemingly hopeless situation in your life?

2 NOW READ JEREMIAH 30–31.

3 Switchback

Have sins ever created walls between you and God? Have you ever wished that you could just start over again? The good news is that God consistently gives you that chance. God consistently offers forgiveness. Scripture is full of stories about God offering a new start.

In Jeremiah 31, God promises a new covenant with Israel and Judah. Unlike the legalistic covenant that God had made with their ancestors, this new covenant will involve the transformation of the people's hearts. "I will put my law within them," God says (31:33). If you need a new start, remember that God always offers new beginnings.

• How do you know when sin is creating a wall between you and God?

 Although Jeremiah gives messages of repentance and judgment, he also has an important prophecy concerning salvation. Read Jeremiah 31 and look for this special message. Study also Exodus 19:3-6; Deuteronomy 7:6-11; Jeremiah 32:37-40; Luke 22:17-20; Hebrews 8:6 and 9:15. What have you learned about Jeremiah's prophecy in Jeremiah 31? How do those verses before and after the Jeremiah passage put it in context? Take a quiz at *amazingbiblerace.com* to earn points.

 4 **Prayer**

When we've wandered, precious God, help us find a new life in you. Amen.

No Faith, No Hope, and All in a Hole
Jeremiah 32–35

 Scouting the Terrain

Trailblazers

- God
- Jeremiah
- King Zedekiah
- King Nebuchadrezzar
- Hanamel
- Baruch
- King Jehoiakim
- The Rechabites

Surrounded by the Babylonian army, the residents of Jerusalem wait. While under siege, no one can safely venture outside the city walls. Imagine the fear in the air. The people can see the foreign army camped outside. The people live off stored-up food and hope that the enemy will go away. (That's what happened a century earlier, when a besieging Assyrian army was destroyed, perhaps by disease. See Isaiah 37:36-38.) In spite of everything, the people believe that God will not let the city fall— no matter how much they have sinned.

During the siege, Jeremiah waits in prison. King Zedekiah believes that the prophet's voice of doom would hurt morale. As the siege continues, however, Zedekiah must face the reality that Jeremiah might be right; so he visits the imprisoned prophet. The king asks questions of, listens to, and sits with the one who has predicted his destruction.

- What emotions, do you think, did Jeremiah feel during the siege of Jerusalem? What emotions, do you think, did King Zedekiah feel?

WEEK
5
◆
DAY
4

The Extra Mile

Reread Chapter 32 very closely. What does Jeremiah do that seems silly, considering both his own situation and the political situation? What makes this strange act an act of hope?

NOW READ JEREMIAH 32–35.

3 Switchback

Amid the Babylonian invasion, many people surely questioned whether God remained faithful to them. Jeremiah tells them that changing God's covenant was as unlikely as changing the times that night and day come. It is easier to stop the world from spinning on its axis than for God to let go of a promise. In other words, God's promises make the world go around.

We can take comfort in God's promise. We can do a pretty good job messing things up sometimes by our own mistakes and sins. Yet there's nothing we can do that will cause God to abandon us.

• When have you doubted God's promises?

• How can we know that God is faithful to God's promises no matter what?

Road Sign

• **Rechabites:** The people in this religious order believed that wilderness living was more faithful than that of the cities. They lived in tents in deserts and didn't drink wine. Jeremiah uses them as an illustration of faithfulness to God.

 Who among your congregation or in your community is in a desperate situation and needs a gesture of hope (similar to Jeremiah's land purchase)? Create a symbol of the hope of God's promises to display in your church or community. Upload a picture or video of your work at *amazingbiblerace.com* for points.

 Prayer

God of Hope, thank you for your faithfulness. Thank you for holding on to us even when we let go of you. Amen.

Jerusalem Under Siege
Jeremiah 36–39

① Scouting the Terrain

As the long siege continues, Jerusalem has run out of bread. Food is scarce. People are beginning to panic. King Zedekiah has not followed Jeremiah's advice, though it becomes increasingly clear that Jeremiah truly knows what God declares. Threatened by impending doom, Zedekiah takes secret counsel once more with Jeremiah. Pay attention to how the king responds to Jeremiah's word.

As the city weakens under the siege, it appears that Jeremiah has been right all along. But even though he suggests a strategy that will preserve the city and its people, the king's officials accuse him of siding with the enemy and throw him into a well.

Trailblazers

- **God**
- **Jeremiah**
- **King Jehoiakim**
- **Baruch**
- **Micaiah**
- **King Zedekiah**
- **Ebed-melech**
- **King Nebuchadrezzar**

• When have you wanted to reject something even though it was true?

• Why, do you think, does Zedekiah decide to consult with Jeremiah again?

②
**NOW READ
JEREMIAH 36–39.**

3 Switchback

Why does God (speaking through Jeremiah) want King Zedekiah to surrender? Isn't it better and more glorious to go down fighting for your homeland? Not in this case. God calls the king and the few remaining unconquered cities of Judah to lay down their weapons, with the promise that Jerusalem, the Temple, and the people will survive. God is not testing whether the people will die for what they believe but whether they'll obey God's commandments and trust that God will take care of them.

• What significance, if any, do you attach to the fact that Jeremiah's life was saved by a foreigner, Ebed-melech the Ethiopian, and not by one of his own people?

Water Break

Whew, another week of Jeremiah is done! It's a long book. Poor Jeremiah had quite a full life of ups and downs (especially downs). But if you keep traveling with him, it will pay off. Hold on for one more week!

4 Prayer

God, grant us the discernment to know when you are speaking to us. Give us the courage to act on your word in all that we do. Amen.

Now What?
Jeremiah 40–43

Scouting the Terrain

Trailblazers

• God
• Jeremiah
• Nebuzaradan
  (captain of
  the guard)
• Gedaliah
• Ishmael
• Johanan
• Azariah

After the Babylonians capture Jerusalem and King Zedekiah, they have the challenge of figuring out what to do with the land they conquered. What will happen to the conquered people, the captured king, and other leaders? Whom do they put in charge? What will they do about the worship practices of the defeated people?

The people of Judah also have to figure out how to respond to life under Babylonian rule. Ishmael, a member of the royal family in Jerusalem, rebels against the conquering Babylonians and kills Gedaliah, the Babylonian governor. Other Judahites flee to Egypt, although God sternly warns them not to.

• How does God want the people of Judah to respond to the Babylonian invasion? Does God want them to flee? to fight back? to obey the Babylonian leaders?

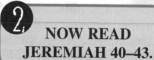

**NOW READ
JEREMIAH 40–43.**

3 Switchback

Have you ever had a friend who would ask for your advice but wouldn't take your advice if it wasn't what he or she wanted to hear? Maybe you concluded that this friend wasn't really looking for advice but for someone to agree with him or her, to validate his or her decision.

Some of the people left in Judah after the Babylonian conquest come to Jeremiah seeking God's guidance. Then they promptly ignore Jeremiah's words. Although they reject the message from God's prophet, they still assume that God will bless their actions.

- What happened when have you asked for someone's advice but really just wanted that person to agree with a decision you had already made?

- Have you ever prayed to God to show you the way when you already knew what you were going to do?

Jeremiah

Racing Tip

In Jeremiah 42:10, God is sorry for the pain that the people have endured. To be sorry suggests guilt or remorse. Does this mean that God made a mistake? God is probably feeling the hurt and anguish of the people, like the parent who says, "This will hurt me more than it hurts you" just before punishing a child. At any rate, this story reveals the depth of God's love and willingness to forgive.

 Prayer

God of wisdom, help us truly listen to you. Empower us to recognize that what we want is not always what you want for us.
Amen.

59

God's Way or the Highway
Jeremiah 44–46

1 Scouting the Terrain

In today's reading, Jeremiah reports addressing "all the Judeans living in the land of Egypt, at Migdol, at Tahpanhes, at Memphis, and in the land of Pathros" (44:1). Such a meeting would have been difficult, since these locations are spread throughout Egypt. Chapters 44–46 begin a series of addresses that Jeremiah makes to the people of Judah who have fled to Egypt in the wake of Babylon's conquest. These addresses tend to follow a pattern. Jeremiah addresses the people, who then reject what Jeremiah has said, bringing further negative consequences on themselves. God consistently offers a way to peace, but the bull-headedness of the people always gets in the way.

Trailblazers

• God
• Jeremiah
• Baruch
• Pharaoh Neco
• King Nebuchadrezzar

• In what ways does God offer us peace and redemption?

• When have you, like the people of Judah, rejected an opportunity to get back on the right track?

2 NOW READ JEREMIAH 44–46.

 Switchback

In Chapter 46, God addresses Egypt with language that sounds like "trash talk":

- "Give Pharaoh, king of Egypt, the name, 'Braggart who missed his chance' " (46:17). Translation: Pharaoh is full of himself.
- "A beautiful heifer is Egypt" (46:20). Translation: Egypt may look nice, but it's just a fat, stupid cow.
- "Even her mercenaries in her midst are like fatted calves" (46:21). Translation: Egypt's best, hired soldiers are slow and lazy.

The language is colorful, and it can help keep your attention. But God's harsh words also make a point to Jeremiah's hearers: Trusting in Egypt, instead of God alone, is just silly.

- Why, do you think, does God use such harsh words to talk about Egypt?

- Why should humans avoid using "trash talk"?

Road Sign

- **"and all the women"** (44:24): Jeremiah addresses "all the people and all the women" (44:24a). Wouldn't *people* include women? While this Scripture may reveal a tendency to devalue the importance of women, it may also have been included to emphasize women. In this case, it was the wives who were making offerings to the "queen of heaven."

Prayer

God of light, illumine our way through your Scriptures. Let your word sink into our hearts, minds, and souls. Amen.

Waking Divine Wrath
Jeremiah 47–49

 Scouting the Terrain

Trailblazers
• God
• Jeremiah

Today's readings focus on prophecies concerning nations and cities surrounding the fallen kingdom of Judah—Moab, Ammon, Edom, and Damascus. While there were clear differences between these neighbors and Judah (in many cases, they also were historical enemies), all were guilty of sins that provoked God's wrath. Among these sins, idolatry was common. And, like Judah, the surrounding kingdoms were guilty of being prideful and failing to care for the poor.

But God's judgment is not the same for all the kingdoms. Pay attention to which countries get a chance to redeem themselves.

• Why, do you think, did God deal differently with these different nations?

• If Jeremiah were to prophesy against our nation and other nations in our world today, what might he say?

• What trends in our society should make faithful Christians cautious?

**NOW READ
JEREMIAH 47–49.**

Switchback

In Jeremiah's time, the leading cause of death among women was childbirth. In fact, only in the past century has modern medicine has removed many of the major risks associated with childbirth. What, then, does it mean when Jeremiah compares Damascus to a woman in labor?

First, the labor that Damascus faces will certainly be painful, as people die and possessions are stolen or burned. Second, Damascus is not promised a new child, a new beginning that would make the pain more bearable. The destruction about to come is like a failed childbirth in which both mother and baby die. Few kinds of emotional pain are greater than the grief that comes when the hope for new life is crushed. That is the depth of the suffering that Jeremiah foretold to Damascus and Judah's other neighbors.

- Jeremiah uses very powerful imagery to convey the level of destruction and suffering on various cities. Which verse provides the most powerful imagery for you? Why?

 Prayer

God of life, guard us from the suffering of the past. Help us endure the suffering of the present. Empower us to reduce the suffering of the future. Amen.

Sweet Redemption
Jeremiah 50–52

 Scouting the Terrain

Trailblazers

- God
- Jeremiah
- Seraiah
- King Zedekiah
- King Nebuchadrezzar
- King Jehoiachin
- King Evil-merodach

Jeremiah 50 brings some of the sweetest news that the people of Judah could imagine: The Babylonians will be conquered. God's people will return to the Promised Land. Best of all, their sins are forgiven. All is forgiven. The long and painful exile is truly at an end.

It had taken 70 years. Generations of children had grown up in a foreign land, knowing Jerusalem only from stories. Now they were going home to the place they had heard so much about. It was certainly something to celebrate.

- How might 70 years of exile in Babylon have affected the people of Judah's faith in God?

- What would be frightening about returning "home" to a place you had never been? What would be exciting?

2. NOW READ JEREMIAH 50–52.

Switchback

The violence in Jeremiah leaves us with persistent and disturbing questions. Among them: Why didn't God use some other way to restore the relationship between God and God's people?

Jeremiah ends by retelling the story of the fall of Jerusalem and subsequent exile. It reminds the reader of the pivotal moments of pain and suffering. Jerusalem was the place, it was believed, where God lived. Losing Jerusalem and the Temple was a sign of the deep separation from God. Calling attention to it again is Jeremiah's way of keeping the exiles from focusing on only the good news of return and forgetting the painful lesson of the past.

• Where do you feel closest to God? How would you feel if you were forced to leave that place or if it were destroyed? What would happen to your relationship with God?

Road Sign

• **Medes** (meeds): Also called Media, this Persian province helped to overthrow the Assyrians in the seventh century and the Babylonians in the eighth century.

Water Break

You've just finished two of the longest books in the Bible and you've walked with God's people during their darkest hour. Unfortunately, we can't lighten the mood as we head into another book attributed to Jeremiah.

 Prayer

God, help us remember the suffering that your people have endured in the past. May these memories bring us closer to you and what you promise your children. Amen.

Poetic Sorrow
Lamentations 1–5

1 Scouting the Terrain

Lamentations is a collection of anguish-filled poetry that screams from the soul. In elegant language, the book reveals the depth of Judah's pain. Sometimes the language shifts into the first person, taking on the identity of Jerusalem and the pain that she endured. When reading Lamentations, pay close attention to the imagery and the extreme emotion. The pain is raw. The author wrestles with God, using language that borders on sarcasm. Lamentations is a straight-from-the-heart book of pain, confession, pleading, and vulnerability.

Trailblazers
- God
- The people of Jerusalem

• How can poetry communicate emotions, particularly painful ones, in ways that other types of literature cannot?

 Each chapter of Lamentations can be characterized as a distinct poem. Study the book as a whole and each chapter separately. With your team, summarize each chapter with a sentence or two. Then take a quiz at *amazingbiblerace.com* to check your analysis of this book.

2 NOW READ LAMENTATIONS 1–5.

Switchback

Lamentations ends as the people of Judah are just beginning their captivity. The siege of Jerusalem has been a horror. Thousands have died of starvation. Mothers have resorted to cooking the bodies of their dead children. The priests of the Temple have been slaughtered. Yet, remarkably, the author of Lamentations can say that God's mercies never come to an end (3:22). The last line, "renew our days as of old—unless you have utterly rejected us and are angry with us beyond measure," puts the ball in God's court. There is nothing left for the people of Judah to do, but wait and see if God, who has forgiven them so many times, will give them one more chance.

• When have you been angry at God? How did you express these emotions?

Road Sign

• **The Lord's "footstool"** (2:1): This is a reference to the ark of the Lord or the Temple.

Lamentations

Prayer

God, renew our days as of old, and help us remember, even in the worst of times, that your love never ends. Amen.

Racing Tip

Greek manuscripts of Lamentations attribute the book to Jeremiah. This attribution is not found in earlier Hebrew versions. Many scholars who have studied the language and style of Lamentations do not think that Jeremiah wrote the book.

Water Break

Way to go! Six weeks down and another six to go! Hang on and read what Ezekiel found himself called to do. have you ever seen skeletons come to life? Read on!

Visions and Voices
Ezekiel 1–5

1 Scouting the Terrain

Where is God? That question haunted the former residents of Judah who were forcibly relocated to Babylon. When we meet Ezekiel, he is among the exiles weeping "by the rivers of Babylon" (Psalm 137:1), wondering why God has allowed foreign enemies to seize control of God's house. Where will the exiles meet God now? When they left their home, had they left God behind too?

Trailblazers

• **God**
• **Ezekiel**

The first chapters of Ezekiel announce that the exiles are not alone. In a spectacular vision, Ezekiel sees God arrive on the scene. God fills him with the Holy Spirit, empowering him to see and tell how God is at work even through Judah's defeat. Ezekiel does unusual things in his visions (such as eating a scroll) and in his everyday life (such as laying siege to a brick). But through it all, Ezekiel communicates God's messages of condemnation and comfort. In this book full of symbols, Ezekiel himself becomes a sign that God is always with us.

• When have you had doubts about whether God was still at work?

• What fears keep you from doing God's will and speaking God's Word?

• What "wicked ways" keep people, communities, and nations today from being faithful to God's will?

2 NOW READ EZEKIEL 1–5.

Racing Tip

Ezekiel may be describing the Ark of the Covenant, an earthly representation of God's heavenly throne in motion, serving God like a chariot—a visual affirmation that God is with the exiles and is not "grounded" in Jerusalem.

3 Switchback

Ezekiel 1 paints a dizzying, whirling scene: Fiery, four-faced creatures fly in all directions at once, through clouds, lightning, and crystal-like radiance, moving on wheels within wheels. Ezekiel can't quite take it all in; it is, he stammers, "the appearance of the likeness of the glory of the LORD" (1:28). If our ride with this prophet starts like that, where will it take us?

As you read, be ready for surprising sights, sounds, and sensory overload. Don't worry about remembering every detail; step back and look at the big picture. Focus on what makes sense; let that help you with the rest.

• Have you, like Ezekiel, ever felt "stunned" by God (3:15)? What happened? How do you put that feeling into words?

Road Sign

• **"Son of man":** God calls Ezekiel "son of man," often translated "mortal" or "human," more than 90 times. Later, Jesus will call himself as the Son of Man, referring to both his humanity and divinity.

Ezekiel

Ezekiel 1 describes in vivid detail Ezekiel's vision of the likeness of the glory of the Lord (verse 28). Using any art medium you and your team choose, create your interpretation of the text. Pay close attention to details in the Scripture. Meditate on the elaborate nature of the vision and consider what Ezekiel must have been feeling in the presence of God's glory. After your artwork is complete, compare and contrast it to other artists' interpretations by searching for online photos. How does studying this passage deepen your understanding of the character of God?

Upload video and/or digital photos of your Ezekiel 1 artwork onto *amazingbiblerace.com* to earn points.

4 Prayer

Loving God, thank you for promising to be with us always and everywhere. Make us living signs of your love for others. Amen.

69

God Takes no Prisoners
Ezekiel 6–10

 Scouting the Terrain

The modern stereotype of a prophet is a wild-eyed character frantically declaring, "The end is near!" What we read about Ezekiel nearly fits that picture. He tells the people of Judah that disaster is coming and that God is behind it.

Judah must learn the hard way about God's authority. Although Ezekiel mentions social injustice a few times (8:17; 9:9), he focuses mainly on idol worship. Can you imagine coming home someday to find your family fawning over some impostor who has replaced you? If you can imagine that, you might have some idea of how much these pagan practices offend God.

Trailblazers

- **God**
- **Ezekiel**
- **People of Judah**
- **Divine executioners**
- **Cherubim**
- **Jaazaniah**
- **"Man clothed in linen"**

• What sorts of idols do people today worship?

• How might social injustice and idolatry really be two sides of the same coin?

 We're reading a lot about God's glory throughout Ezekiel. What is God's glory? How is it portrayed in Scripture? Dig into an online Bible and do a word search for *God's glory*. Once you've hunted through the Word, take a quiz about God's glory at *amazingbiblerace.com* for points.

③ Switchback

NOW READ EZEKIEL 6–10.

The vision of God commanding the slaughter of Jerusalem's inhabitants is deeply disturbing. Even Ezekiel is shocked. The prophet pleads for God to show mercy. God's judgment, however, is as relentless as the people's sin. Yet the "man clothed in linen"—a priest or an angel—provides a glimpse of grace. He marks the foreheads of those who have remained faithful. As lamb's blood on the doorposts identified the children of Israel spared from death in Egypt (Exodus 12:21-23), this mark, which looks like an X—identifies those now spared.

• In what ways do we, in the church today, mark people as children of God?

• In your daily living, how do you show that you have been marked as one who belongs to God?

Ezekiel

Road Signs

• **"From the wilderness to Riblah"** (6:14): At the height of its power, Israel stretched from the southwestern desert wilderness to the town of Riblah in the north. The promised destruction will cover this entire area.

• **"This image of jealousy"** (8:5): Ezekiel refers to an unspecified pagan image at an entrance to the Temple that provoked God to feel intolerant of the people's disloyalty.

• **"Weeping for Tammuz"** (8:14): Tammuz was a Babylonian fertility god who, according to myth, died when the dry season began and returned to life—aided by mourners' tears—when the rainy season started.

④ Prayer

Righteous God, in the midst of constant temptation to chase after idols, keep us strong in faith. Amen.

The Divine Plan B
Ezekiel 11–15

1 Scouting the Terrain

"My computer crashed!" It's a common lament in our tech-saturated age. Too bad for you if you haven't saved your work when a power surge or virus strikes! God and Judah's sacred covenant relationship has crashed. Like a computer worm, idolatry infected Judah's life, beginning with its leaders and replicating until the whole society was corrupted. Ezekiel's visions show God performing a radical "reboot." But God isn't starting from scratch. God has a "backup" in the "remnant of Israel"—those who have been taken to Babylon.

This remnant represents hope for the future, but not because of any purity of its own. Even though the exiles, too, tend toward idolatry, God gives them the opportunity to repent. God promises to bring them back home and give them "one heart" that beats for God alone (11:19). When God repairs the broken relationship with them, the people will understand that their exile was part of God's plan. The "system" will be up and running—this time, once and for all (compare Jeremiah 31:33-34).

Trailblazers

• **God**
• **Ezekiel**
• **People of Jerusalem**
• **Jaazaniah**
• **Pelatiah**
• **Cherubim**

• When have you been able to see how something bad fits into God's plan for good?

• What is the difference between a "heart of stone" and a "heart of flesh" (11:19)?

2 NOW READ EZEKIEL 11–15.

③ Switchback

Every time we go through grocery store checkout lines, we see in the tabloids examples of so-called "prophecy" from psychics and astrologers. Sometimes it's worth a good laugh. But false prophecy in biblical times was nothing to snicker at. Men and women who say that they speak for God make a bold claim and had better be prepared for the consequences when people listen to them. God's condemnation of false prophets reminds us to make sure that we know God's will whenever we speak in God's name.

Notice also that true prophecy isn't necessarily about telling the future. While Ezekiel and some other legitimate prophets do make accurate predictions, most prophecy tells the truth from God's point of view about the here and now. Prophecy often is interpreting the present from an eternal perspective.

• Whom would you consider a present-day prophet?

• How are Christians called to be prophets?

Road Sign

• **Whitewash** (13:10-16): This paint, developed hundreds of years ago, was an inexpensive and somewhat temporary wall coating. (Mark Twain's famous character Tom Sawyer tricked other boys into doing his punishment of having to whitewash a fence.) The word has become a synonym for glossing over faults, hiding the truth, or otherwise covering up unflattering details.

Ezekiel

④ Prayer

God, thank you for loving us enough to call us to repentance. Amen.

Creative Truth-Telling
Ezekiel 16–20

1) Scouting the Terrain

When kids become frightened while watching a scary movie, adults tell them, "Don't worry; it's just a story." That reassurance might comfort a child scared by a monster flick. But even made-up stories can contain troubling truth.

In today's reading, Ezekiel complains: "GOD, everyone says that I'm just making up stories" (20:49, paraphrase). Ezekiel uses a lot of symbols when he speaks. For example, Chapter 17's story of the vine is about Judah's King Zedekiah, who rebels against Nebuchadnezzar of Babylon (the first eagle), in favor of Egyptian pharaoh Psammetichus II (the second eagle). These texts are stories, but they're not fiction.

Ezekiel speaks more plainly elsewhere. God's declaration of strict justice in Chapter 18 shows what's at stake. If the remnant can hear the truth in the prophet's stories and repent, it will live.

- Like Ezekiel, Jesus used narratives to convey God's message. What advantages might stories have over other ways of sharing God's Word? What risks might stories carry?

Trailblazers

- God
- Ezekiel
- Kings Nebuchadnezzar, Zedekiah, Jehoiachin, Jehoahaz, Jehoiakim
- Psammetichus II

WEEK
7
◆
DAY
4

2) NOW READ EZEKIEL 16–20.

Extra Mile

Look at how God called the prophets Isaiah (6:1-13), Jeremiah (1:4-19), and Ezekiel (1:1–3:11). Answer the following questions regarding each of them so that you can compare their experiences:

- Is pain involved?
- Does the person immediately accept the call, or does he resist in some way? If so, how?
- Does the prophet receive any supernatural powers?
- Is the prophet somehow cleansed or purified? If so, how?
- Does the story describe God? If so, how?

3 Switchback

Ezekiel 16, which compares God's judgment of Jerusalem to a husband's punishment of an adulterous wife, may trouble some readers. It's easy to brush off the passage as being merely symbolic. But we've already seen that symbolism can't be dismissed so easily. There's no way to deny that this text uses images of sexually charged violence to convey its message. This is due in part to its historical and cultural context. In those days, stripping and stoning were not uncommon punishments for adultery (see, for example, Deuteronomy 22:20-24). And marriage was not expected to be an equal partnership like it is today. It was more like a treaty between two unequal nations in which the lesser nation pledges loyalty and obedience in exchange for protection.

Knowledge of the cultural context doesn't make this Scripture any easier to digest. But remember that, despite this violent imagery, God never stopped loving God's people.

• What does the language and imagery in this Scripture tell you about God's reaction to Judah's unfaithfulness?

Road Sign

• **Sister cities** (16:46-61): Samaria was the capital of Israel (the northern kingdom), and was conquered by the Assyrian Empire in 722 B.C., about 125 years before Ezekiel's preaching (see 2 Kings 17). Sodom was the city destroyed for its wickedness (Genesis 19).

Racing Tip

Aren't we saved by grace? (18:20-24) Christians affirm that none of our works can earn us salvation. But we also believe that we are saved so that we may do good works. God's message in Ezekiel 18:20—"The person who sins shall die"—may seem to contradict the teaching of salvation by grace through faith. This chapter, however, more likely deals with the impending fall of Jerusalem.

4 Prayer

God, our imperfect words can never fully express your way with us. Yet strengthen us to keep telling the world of your never-ending love. Amen.

King of All the Earth
Ezekiel 21–25

1 Scouting the Terrain

As the nations surrounding Judah are busy gloating over Jerusalem's fall, the Babylonian juggernaut keeps steamrolling through the ancient world. But these violent events are not *just happening*. God is behind the scenes, bringing divine order out of what seems like chaos.

Trailblazers

- God
- Ezekiel
- King Nebuchadnezzar
- King Zedekiah
- Oholah = Samaria
- Oholibah = Jerusalem

Chapter 21 is Act 1 of the redemptive drama whose second act you read about in Isaiah 40–55. Here, God uses Nebuchadnezzar of Babylon to take the remnant of God's people into the exile from which Cyrus of Persia will release them 50 years later. Babylon is God's sword of punishment, although it is not safe from future punishment itself. In Chapter 25, a series of God's judgments against other nations begins.

The God of Israel is not the God of Israel alone. As the psalm-singer affirmed, "God is the king of all the earth.... God is king over the nations" (Psalm 47:7a, 8a). Our individual sins are serious, but so are the sins of the nations. Jesus promised that, when he returns, he will gather and judge "the nations" (Matthew 25:32).

- Of what sins does our nation need to repent? What would national repentance look like?

WEEK
7
◆
DAY
5

2 NOW READ EZEKIEL 21–25.

3 Switchback

Ezekiel again uses graphic language to describe the sin and punishment of Israel and Judah. The text tells the tale of Oholah ("she of the tent" = Samaria, capital of the former northern kingdom) and Oholibah ("my tent is in her" = Jerusalem, capital of the southern kingdom), two lustful sisters whose promiscuity leads them both to ruin. We can perhaps find reassurance in the fact that this story would have been shocking to its original audience too. The ancient exiles did not, of course, have twenty-first-century ideas about gender roles or physical abuse, but the story's angry tone would have startled them. It was meant to jolt them into taking the sin of idolatry seriously.

- How seriously do you take the sin of idolatry in your society and in your own life?

Road Signs

- **Divination** (21:18-23): This is the false system of trying to predict the future, in other words, to figure out divine will.
- **Inspecting the liver:** Some ancient people believed that they could foretell the future by looking at the configurations and markings of a sheep liver.

Ezekiel

Like other prophets, Ezekiel used symbolic actions to speak God's message. As a team, design a symbolic action that you can perform (1) safely and legally and (2) in public that will speak a truth from Scripture to your community. Make a video or take digital photos of your team performing this symbolic action and upload them to *amazingbiblerace.com* for points.

Water Break

Ezekiel is not for the squeamish. Congratulations on sticking with him this far. Rejoice that you have only one more week of the Book of Ezekiel.

 ## Prayer

God, we are sorry for the ways we break your law and turn away from your love. Amen.

The Long Fall From Pride
Ezekiel 26–30

1 Scouting the Terrain

Today's chapters continue with God's judgment of nations other than Judah, and the harsh spotlight falls on Phoenicia (the area of modern Lebanon) and Egypt. Both societies ranked among the most advanced of the ancient world. Phoenician sailors journeyed to the farthest-known reaches of the earth. The Phoenician alphabet was a precursor to our own. Phoenicia's two greatest city-states, Tyre and Sidon, dominated Mediterranean trade. Egypt, of course, still amazes us as one of the wealthiest civilizations of the ages.

Trailblazers
• God
• Ezekiel

But neither of these powerhouses stayed at the top forever. In the 8th century B.C., Phoenicia was incorporated into the Assyrian Empire. Less than a century later, the Assyrians would temporarily take control of Egypt. Both nations would also be attacked by the Babylonians. God told Ezekiel that the declines of Phoenicia and Egypt were the direct result of divine intervention. These nations trusted too much in their might and money. The king of Tyre had even proudly declared himself a god. So God finally brought these nations low. No less guilty of idolatry than Judah, the Phoenicians and Egyptians share Judah's fate.

• How do nations behave arrogantly today?

• How, do you think, does God judge nations today?

2 NOW READ EZEKIEL 26–30.

3 Switchback

While the Hebrew Bible focuses on Israel's identity as God's chosen people, God is still in relationship with the entire world. In Ezekiel 28:11-19, for instance, God refers to Tyre as a former resident of the Garden of Eden. The symbolic language suggests that God feels real grief over Tyre's behavior and coming punishment. Tyre had a part to play in God's good plan for the world. Unfortunately, like Jerusalem, Tyre rejected that role, denying that its prosperity came from God, pretending that it was self-sufficient.

Today, we should continue to affirm the biblical truth that God rules over all the nations and that God's love is available to all people. All nations have a place in "the garden of God" (Ezekiel 28:13).

- How can Christian congregations and individuals concretely speak the message of God's love for all nations in the world today?

Ezekiel

4 Prayer

God, save us from unhealthful pride, and lead us to love and serve you alone. Amen.

And the Walls Came Tumbling Down
Ezekiel 31–35

 Scouting the Terrain

A dozen years after the exiles' deportation, the update from home finally arrives: Jerusalem has fallen. Even though the exiles should have known that this destruction was coming, the news still packs quite a punch. Ezekiel has been a "sentinel," relaying God's message. He has called the people to repent; he has identified this moment to receive a new beginning from God.

Trailblazers

• God
• Ezekiel
• Pharaoh
• Assyrians
• Edom

Some people will respond favorably; others won't. Regardless, Ezekiel has done his duty. The day's headlines validate what he has been saying since that incredible vision by the banks of the Chebar. And now that they've heard the bad news, the exiles are more than ready to hear the good. From these chapters onward, Ezekiel has less to say about what has gone wrong and more about how God will make things right.

• Do you tend to look more to the past or to the future? Why?

• When have you had to give someone bad news? What happened?

2. NOW READ EZEKIEL 31–35.

❸ Switchback

Shadowy "Sheol" appears in these chapters several times. God chops down the mighty tree, a symbol of Egypt; and it falls into Sheol (31:14-15), where the earth's "majestic nations" (32:18) eventually end up (32:21-30). What is this place? It's definitely not "heaven" as Christians think of it; but it's definitely not "hell," either.

To ancient Israelites, Sheol was a gloomy, neither-here-nor-there place to which all of the dead go. In today's chapters, God mentions only the too-proud nations of the past as winding up in Sheol; but Assyria, Elam, and the rest are only sharing what, according to most of the Hebrew Bible, is awaiting everyone.

Next week, in the Book of Daniel, we will catch a glimpse of something different; and in Leg 5 we will see that "something different" even more clearly on the first Easter morning.

• When you think about life after death, what images come to mind?

Racing Tip

Before he became Israel's king, David was a shepherd. Moses, too, had been a shepherd when he received God's call. Understandably, then, ancient Israel sometimes described its leaders as shepherds. Ezekiel 34, however, paints a picture of really rotten shepherds who lead those in their care astray. As a result, God promises to handle the shepherding from now on (34:12). When Jesus calls himself the Good Shepherd (John 10:11), he is drawing on imagery such as that in Ezekiel's prophecy.

Prayer

Savior, like a shepherd lead us; much we need Thy tender care.
—Dorothy A. Thrupp, 1836 (attributed)

God's Surgical Skills
Ezekiel 36–39

 Scouting the Terrain

In today's chapters, God promises to give Israel a heart transplant. You might remember that, through Jeremiah, God delivered this glum prognosis: "The heart is devious above all else" (Jeremiah 17:9). So God is left with only one choice: to remove the people's "heart of stone"—a heart so scarred over with sin that it can no longer really beat—and replace it with a "heart of flesh"—a fresh heart capable of loving and obeying God.

This transplant is, in fact, an infusion of God's own Spirit (Ezekiel 36:27). Ezekiel's famous vision of dry, scattered bones coming to life (37:1-14) depicts the life-giving result of God's cardiac care. The exiles, who felt as good as dead, would live again and could anticipate a future relationship with God—not because of anything they did but because of the operation of the Holy Spirit within and among them.

Trailblazers

• God
• Ezekiel
• Gog

• What evidence of God's "heart transplant" do you see in your life and in the life of your youth group or congregation?

• In the world, in your community, in your church, and in your relationships, what "dry bones" need to feel God's Spirit blowing over them today?

2 **NOW READ EZEKIEL 36–39.**

③ Switchback

Readers have long puzzled over the identity of Gog (38:2). Who is this future enemy of the restored Israel, whom God alone will defeat? People have proposed a variety of candidates. But the prophecy really expresses Jewish thinking about the end of history, when God would intervene decisively to defeat evil.

Clearly, the exiles felt that hostile forces dominated their world. Gog rears an ugly head in the book of Revelation too, so the early Christian communities to whom John of Patmos addressed feared Gog as well. In both cases, Gog is a striking symbol of the world's opposition to God's good will for it. Gog's defeat is a ringing affirmation of God's power and rule.

• Where today do you see spiritual warfare between God and Gog?

Ezekiel's vision in Chapter 37 has relevance for today's believers. Read about the Valley of Dry Bones along with Ephesians 2:1-10. How are the two passages related? What does this mean for your Christian journey? Once you've studied the two passages side-by-side, take a quiz at *amazingbiblerace.com* to earn points.

Catch Your Breath

As Ezekiel explains, God has a reputation to protect (see 36:22-23). Had the exiles been allowed to perish, the world would have assumed that the God of Israel was powerless. Had the people been allowed to go on "profaning" God's name through their sinful ways, the world would have assumed that the God of Israel was no better than any member of the pagan pantheon. Yes, God loves the people; but these chapters remind us that what we do reflects, well or poorly, on the God in whom we profess belief.

Prayer

Lord, raise us up by your Spirit, that our hearts might always beat with passion to do your work. Amen.

Home Is Where the Worship Is
Ezekiel 40–44

 Scouting the Terrain

God carries Ezekiel off to Jerusalem "in visions." A man, likely an angel, gives Ezekiel a grand tour of a new Temple.

Trailblazers

- **God**
- **Ezekiel**
- **Man whose "appearance shone like bronze"**

The detailed descriptions of the Temple may seem boring. But Ezekiel's original audience would have heard only good news. If God is returning home from exile (43:1-5), then so are they. This lengthy vision is a promise that nothing, not even the people's sins, will ultimately separate them from God.

- When are you most glad to be at home? What positive experiences do you have at home that you have nowhere else?

WEEK
8
◇
DAY
4

- The Temple represented God's presence to ancient Israel. What is a meaningful sign or symbol of God's presence for you? Why?

 The final chapters of Ezekiel are largely concerned with worship space. The physical arrangement of the Temple in Jerusalem was intended to reflect spiritual realities. The space in which we worship affects how we worship.

As a team, tour your congregation's primary worship space. Note as many details as you can. What purposes, practical or otherwise, do the furnishings, decorations, and so forth serve? How well does the space encourage people to worship God? Videotape and deliver a presentation for your congregation about the relationship between worship and the space. Make recommendations to the pastor and/or worship director about creating a more worshipful environment. Then upload your video onto *amazingbiblerace.com* for points.

Switchback

Ezekiel's vision of the new Temple is all about defining holiness. The root meaning of *holiness* is "otherness." God is holy by definition, because God transcends the world. So when God chooses to enter the world, the world must somehow be made to accommodate God. Sacred space must be carved out. The precise measurements that Ezekiel's angelic guide uses to stake out the Temple and its grounds create the boundaries that, in a sense, "protect" the people from God's holy presence. We must enter into God's holy presence with reverence, slowly and deliberately.

Then, bit by bit, we begin to become holy and "different" ourselves. We become carriers of God's holy presence into the world that God so loves.

- In what ways do you take time to enter slowly and deliberately into God's holy presence?

- How are you carrying God's holy presence into the world with you today?

NOW READ EZEKIEL 40–44.

Road Sign

- **"Levitical priests of the family of Zadok"** (43:19): Zadok was a priest who rose to prominence during the reigns of David and Solomon. Zadok's descendants served as high priests in Jerusalem before and after the exile.

Ezekiel

 Prayer

Holy God, fill our hearts so that we may share in your holiness as we share with others your love. Amen.

The River of Life Flows On
Ezekiel 45–48

1 Scouting the Terrain

Ezekiel's prophecy began beside the Chebar River in Babylon (1:1). It ends by a river, too—one that flows from the restored Temple in Jerusalem (47:1-12). When it flows into the Dead Sea, those salty waters become fresh, enabling life to thrive: Where the river flows, every living creature will live (47:9). It almost sounds like a fairy-tale ending.

Trailblazers
- God
- Ezekiel
- Tribes of Israel

But the return to the land was difficult. The work of rebuilding, during Ezra and Nehemiah's days, proved tough and dangerous; Judah (later called Judea under Roman rule) did not become the center of global influence that prophets envisioned.

But the hope remained. Ezekiel's message remained strong in the people's memory—so strong that, centuries later, believers continued to envision their future in his terms. From the throne of God, these believers proclaimed, will flow a river of life, along the banks of which are trees yielding fruit and leaves "for the healing of the nations" (Revelation 21:2).

• What images from Ezekiel will stay with you most? Why?

• How will you demonstrate today your trust in God's promises for the future?

2 NOW READ EZEKIEL 45–48.

3 Switchback

What does the name of your city or town mean? Is it named after a great person of the past—Washington, Lincoln, Jefferson? Does the name reflect local history, perhaps, or geography—Sioux City, Butte, Atlantic City? Does it take the name of an abstract virtue—Philadelphia, for example, "the city of brotherly love"? Until the final verse of his prophecy, Ezekiel has not told us the name of the city to which God has taken him in these last eight chapters. Of course, his vision takes place in Jerusalem. But nowhere does that name appear. Instead, at the close of the vision, Jerusalem receives a new name: "The LORD is There" (48:35). The name testifies to the truth that defines the city's existence.

• If God were to rename your city, what name would you hope for?

• What can you do to help make your city worthy of that new name?

As Christians, we believe that, in the Spirit of Jesus Christ, God is always with us—and with our cities. With your team and one adult leader, document with a camera or videocamera all glimpses of the "glory of the LORD" (43:4) that you see in your city. Upload your video and/or photos at *amazingbiblerace.com* for points.

Water Break

You've just read some of the most difficult but also most rewarding parts of the Old Testament. You've heard God's call to holy living—and God's promise to give us the new spirit we need to answer the call.

4 Prayer

Heal us, O God, that we may bring healing to a wounded world. Amen.

What Are You Willing to Do to Fit In?
Daniel 1–5

1 Scouting the Terrain

Trailblazers

- **God**
- **Daniel (Belteshazzar)**
- **King Nebuchadnezzar**
- **King Jehoiakim**
- **Ashpenaz**
- **Hananiah (Shadrach)**
- **Mishael (Meshach)**
- **Azariah (Abednego)**
- **Palace master**
- **Magicians, enchanters, sorcerers, Chaldeans**
- **Arioch**
- **King Belshazzar**

Like Ezekiel, Daniel was deported from Jerusalem after Babylon captured the city in 597 B.C. But Daniel was placed into a position of privilege. When we first read about him and his three friends, they are being groomed for royal service, receiving a top-notch, Babylonian education and a royal meal plan to go with it.

These young men learn the local language and even answer to new names, but they reject the pagan menu. It's the first of several times in which they walk a fine line between fitting in and staying faithful to who they are: God's chosen people, called to model holiness to the rest of the world. Through gripping stories and startling visions, the Book of Daniel challenges us to keep faith with the God who always keeps faith with us.

- Have you ever been tempted to compromise your faith so that others would accept you? If so, what happened?

- How do you decide how much you, as a Christian, can participate in secular culture?

2 NOW READ DANIEL 1–5.

3 Switchback

You've already met Jacob and Joseph, both of whom God spoke to in dreams. Daniel is another dreamer. He believes that "there is a God in heaven who reveals mysteries" in dreams (2:28).

In episodes that remind readers of Joseph and Pharaoh (Genesis 41:1-40), Daniel interprets Nebuchadnezzar's nightmares (Daniel 2:1-45; 4:1-27). With the fast pace of our lives today, the hours we spend in sleep may be the perfect time for God to get our attention.

• Has God ever spoken to you through a dream? If so, what happened? How did you respond?

Road Signs

• **Feet of clay** (2:33, 41-43): Nebuchadnezzar's nightmare is the source of this common phrase, meaning that even the "highest and mightiest" are only human and liable to fall.

• **"And the fourth has the appearance of a god"** (3:25): So who is that mysterious fourth fellow hanging out in the fiery furnace? The book's original audience understood the fourth man to be an angel. Since the early days of the church, however, some Christians have understood him to be Jesus.

• **The writing on the wall** (5:5): When we say that we can "read the writing on the wall," we mean that we can plainly see the truth. Daniel sees the truth about Belshazzar: The king's days are numbered.

• **Chaldeans** (1:6): When referring to advisors that King Nebuchadnezzar relied on, this is another name for "astrologers." In the general sense, however, Chaldeans were an ancient Semitic people who were otherwise known as Babylonians.

Daniel

4 Prayer

God, reveal what is deeply hidden in darkness. Shine light into our lives. Amen.

If Daniel Ran the Zoo
Daniel 6–9

1 Scouting the Terrain

As you read today's chapters, you may feel as though you're reading a Dr. Seuss story. A winged lion? A three-tusked bear? A flying, four-headed leopard? A huge beast with 10 horns? Dr. Seuss might not even know what to call *that*. God calls that beast, and the rest, doomed. God bangs the gavel and sentences these beasts to destruction. God then elevates "one like a human being" or "son of man" (7:13)—to a position of everlasting authority. Christians believe that Jesus called himself "Son of Man," in part, to identify himself as the one from heaven who executes God's judgment and establishes God's justice.

In Daniel's dreams, the beasts symbolize powerful kingdoms brought low. For us, the beasts can represent any force opposed to God. The sight of their defeat assures us that, in the end, God's good will shall be done.

Trailblazers

• **Daniel**
• **King Darius**
• **King Belshazzar**

• What "beasts" do you see stalking your community and your life?

• Even the angels who bring Daniel glimpses of God's ultimate victory ask, "How long?" (8:13). When do you ask God that question?

2 NOW READ DANIEL 6–9.

3 Switchback

If your congregation includes a unison prayer of confession in worship, you may have wondered, "Why am I saying this? I didn't do this stuff!" Well, Daniel hasn't personally committed any of the sins he prays about in 9:4-19, either.

Daniel's prayer sets a standard for later Jewish prayers of confession by using the first-person plural when listing various prohibited activities. In both Old and New Testaments, God's people are one people. Community identity shapes individual identity. Although Daniel is righteous in his own life, he acknowledges guilt because he belongs to God's people.

In our unison confession, we admit that all humanity is trapped in sin—and, on all humanity's behalf, pray, as did Daniel, for deliverance.

• If God already knows our sins as individuals and as God's people; and if God is gracious and forgiving—"slow to anger and abounding in steadfast love" (Psalm 103:8)—why should we bother to confess?

 The Babylonians "trained" Israelite men to enter the king's service (Chapter 1) by having them study of language and literature as well as dine on royal food and drink. How are language, literature, food, and drink used to shape our beliefs? Why would Daniel consider the food and drink defiling and refuse to partake of them?

Interview someone who has undergone rigorous training, such military or police, about conforming his or her habits to his or her employer's demands.

Later, discuss with your group how Daniel's situation relates to yours. You may not be training for any special job, but you may be asked to compromise your Christian beliefs in today's culture. Record a video diary of the interview (be sure to get his or her permission) and your thoughts; then upload it to *amazingbiblerace.com* for points.

Daniel

 Prayer

Great and awesome God, we have sinned and done wrong. Hear our prayer and forgive. Amen.

Every Hero Needs a Villain
Daniel 10–12

1 Scouting the Terrain

If King Antiochus IV were a movie character, he would have topped even Darth Vader and Hannibal Lecter on a list of most villainous movie villains. When he took control of the Seleucid kingdom (175 B.C.), he auctioned the Jewish high priesthood to the highest bidder. He made practicing the Jewish religion punishable by death. He enslaved and slaughtered thousands of people. He erected an altar to Zeus in the Temple in Jerusalem, which he further defiled with pig's blood. As a final touch, Antiochus named himself Epiphanes, which means "God appears." Without mentioning Antiochus by name, Daniel 11:36 describes the ruler's audacity.

If people could worship Zeus in the Temple, many of God's people must have been distressed about the future. But no matter how bleak the political situation in Judah got, the people could always find hope in God's promises.

Trailblazers

- **Daniel**
- **King Cyrus**
- **"A man clothed in linen"**
- **Michael the archangel**
- **King Antiochus IV**

• Have you ever wished for God to step in and set our troubled world right? How do you deal with those thoughts and feelings?

2 NOW READ DANIEL 10–12.

3 Switchback

Daniel is an example of how being loved by God isn't all "warm fuzzies" and "spiritual highs." Christians today may forget that to be God's beloved means to have been entrusted with God's sometimes terrifying but always terrifically important message for the world. After all, Jesus was also identified as God's beloved; and by accepting that identity, he accepted the cross. A special relationship with God brings special responsibility.

- How is your identity as a beloved child of God a burden as well as a blessing?

Road Sign

- **"Many of those who sleep"** (12:1-3): Daniel 12 includes the only unambiguous reference in the Hebrew Bible to the doctrine of the resurrection of the dead. The idea that God would raise individuals from death for judgment seems to have surfaced in the second century B.C., as Jews suffered at Antiochus's hands. Not all Jews accepted the idea of a resurrection: In the New Testament, we read that the Sadducees, for example, rejected it.

Daniel

Water Break

Congratulations on finishing the last of the major prophets. Up next are 12 much shorter, but no less challenging, prophetic books.

 Outline the Book of Daniel according to its two different types of material: historical narratives and visions. When your outline is finished, take a quiz online at *amazingbiblerace.com* to check your work.

 4 Prayer

God, when anyone or anything else dares to claim loyalty, we owe only to you. Keep us faithful. Amen.

A Match Made in Heaven
Hosea 1–7

1 Scouting the Terrain

A "match made in heaven" is a seemingly perfect romantic relationship. But the prophet Hosea's marriage, although "made in heaven," was anything but. In one of the strangest sets of instructions ever given to a prophet, God commands Hosea to marry Gomer, knowing that she will cheat on him (1:2). She bears three children, but the last two may or may not be Hosea's (see 2:4-5). Gomer's behavior was grounds for divorce, but Hosea continues to love her (3:1-3).

Through Hosea, who lived in the northern kingdom of Israel in the 8th century B.C.), God charges Israel with infidelity. Led astray by their priests and princes, the people have been looking to pagan fertility gods and foreign powers for security. Like prophets after him, Hosea views Israel's impending defeat as the consequence of its idolatry. But most of all, the book is a statement of God's deep love for Israel. God wants the people for God's own, and will not be satisfied until Israel comes back.

Trailblazers

- God
- Hosea
- Gomer
- Jezreel
- Lo-ruhamah
- Lo-ammi

WEEK
9
◇
DAY
4

• Have you ever experienced a broken heart? If so, how does that experience affect your reading of Hosea?

2 NOW READ HOSEA 1–7.

94

③ Switchback

Imagine going through life with names like Hosea's kids had. Clearly, the names carry symbolic meaning. Two illustrate God's refusal to spare the people: Lo-ruhamah ("not to be pitied") and Lo-ammi ("not my people"). The first name, Jezreel, calls attention to Israel's rebellious and bloody past, since Naboth's vineyard, which King Ahab and Queen Jezebel schemed to steal, was in the valley of Jezreel.

But God also promises name changes: "Not my people" becomes "children of the living God"; Jezreel becomes "great shall be the day of Jezreel." *Jezreel* means "God sows." God will "re-plant" the people after punishing them; and they will in the end hear words of grace: "Oh, call your brothers 'My people,' and your sisters 'Lovingly Accepted.'"

• If you were to choose a new name to symbolize your relationship with God, what name would you choose and why?

Road Sign

• **Ephraim** (EE-fray-im) (4:17): This is another name for the northern kingdom, Israel. The northern kingdom's first ruler, Jeroboam I, came from the territory of Ephraim.

Take me out to the ball, uh, Bible game! The Book of Hosea is first up to bat in this special Minor Prophet League. Today you'll begin to read the "Minor Prophets." Check out *amazingbiblerace.com* to find the Minor Prophets Scorecard. It's a special hurdle that we've designed just for you so that you can keep all of the "player stats" straight. Hit a home run (and earn points) when you fill out the entire scorecard.

Pace Pusher

Memorize Hosea 6:6. Jesus quotes this verse (in Matthew 9:13) to criticize religious leaders who let overly scrupulous concern for the letter of God's Law stand in the way of fulfilling the Law's ultimate aim of love.

④ Prayer

Loving God, guard our hearts, that we may never give them away to anyone but you. Amen.

Hosea

A Window Into God's Heart
Hosea 8–14

1 Scouting the Terrain

Modern medical technology allows doctors to look into the human heart as never before. Hosea gets to look into something even more marvelous. He is allowed to look into the heart of God. In anguished love, the anguished love good mothers and fathers feel when their children rebel, God cries out: "My people are bent on turning away from me....How can I give you up, Ephraim? How can I hand you over, O Israel?" (11:7, 8). God resolves that punishment will not be the last word. The last word will be love.

Christians sometimes mistakenly talk of "the Old Testament God of wrath" and "the New Testament God of love." Hosea teaches us the truth: "The Holy One in [our] midst" (11:9), the God-with-us in Jesus (Matthew 1:23; John 1:14), has a heart that always beats in love.

• How does the prophecy of Hosea illustrate the common saying that the opposite of love is not hate but apathy, just not caring?

• How does the resurrection of Jesus Christ confirm that God's last word is always love?

2 NOW READ HOSEA 8–14.

③ Switchback

In C. S. Lewis's *The Lion, the Witch, and the Wardrobe*, Mr. Beaver tells the Pevensie children about Aslan the great lion: " 'Course he isn't safe. But he's good. He's the King, I tell you."

In the same way, the Holy One of Israel is a lion—not safe or tame but good. In Hosea, the image of God as lion communicates both God's judgment of and God's restoration of the people.

The image will appear again in the Book of Revelation. However, when the Revelation author, John, hears in his vision about the divine lion, he sees the lion revealed as a lamb (Revelation 5:6), who judges, conquers, and rules—not by brute strength but by the strength of love.

Road Signs

- **Scenes of the crimes:** "The days of Gibeah" (9:9; 10:9) were the bad old days near the end of the time of the judges, when "all the people did what was right in their own eyes" (Judges 21:25); so they usually ended up doing what was wrong.
- **Calf of Beth-aven** (10:5)**:** is a second golden calf (remember Exodus 32; see 1 Kings 12:25-33), built at Bethel.
- **Admah and Zeboiim** (zuh-BOY-im) (11:8)**:** These are two wicked cities that were destroyed along with Sodom and Gomorrah (Genesis 19).

- When you think about God, do you treat God more as a lion or as a lamb? How might the other image increase your understanding of and love for God?

Water Break

The three most frequently repeated words in the journals of famous explorers Lewis and Clark are these: "We pressed on." So press on. The remaining 11 prophets may be called "minor," but some major truth awaits you!

④ Prayer

O God, call us back to you when we wander; empower us to blossom with love toward you and justice toward all people. Amen.

Hosea

A Bug-Eyed Army of Destruction
Joel 1–3

1 Scouting the Terrain

Brood X. That's the ominous name for the billions of cicadas that emerge from the ground to swarm over the eastern United States every 17 years. When they last appeared, in 2004, they covered everything in some areas.

Trailblazers
• God
• Joel

Joel lived through an infestation of locusts in Judah in the late 6th or early 5th century B.C. He saw them as an invading army from God, sent to punish God's people for their sin. Joel doesn't specify what the people did wrong, but he urges them to do what's right.

Joel's prophecy does not mean that we should label all natural disasters as expressions of God's wrath. But God can work through natural disasters to bring people closer to God. But why wait for calamity to strike? As you read Joel, answer God's summons: "Return to me with all your heart" (2:12). Don't wait until there's trouble. Renew your commitment to God today!

• When, if ever, has a natural disaster shaken your faith in God?

• When, if ever, has a natural disaster moved you or someone you know closer to God?

2 NOW READ JOEL 1–3.

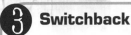

③ Switchback

Joel takes the locust plague as a warning sign of an even greater crisis to come: the Day of the Lord. Like Amos, Joel envisions this future time, when God will intervene to exercise fully God's righteous rule, as a dark day of destruction.

Still, Joel declares that God remains "a refuge for his people" even though "the heavens and the earth shake" (3:16), and relays the promise, "Then everyone who calls on the name of the LORD shall be saved" (2:32). What's more, God promises to "pour out" the Holy Spirit "on all flesh" (2:28). Prophecy—the ability to see and understand the world through God's eyes—will no longer be a spiritual gift restricted to a special few. All of the people will prophesy, just as Moses had longed for them to do so long ago (see Numbers 11:29).

Christians believe that Joel's words were fulfilled on the first Pentecost after Jesus' resurrection. The apostle Peter quotes Joel in Acts 2:16-21, telling his audience that, when Jesus was raised, the "day of the Lord" dawned.

Road Sign
- **Valley of Jehoshaphat** (3:2-14): While the text may refer to a valley named after King Jehoshaphat, ruler of Judah in the early 9th century B.C., it may also be a symbolic place and not an actual spot. The name Jehoshaphat means "The LORD establishes justice," which is exactly what God does at this place.

- When have you been particularly aware that God's light still shines in darkness?

④ Prayer
God, create in us new, contrite hearts that we may obtain from you perfect forgiveness. Amen.

Don't forget to enter Joel's "stats" on your Minor League Prophets Scorecard.

Take a Good Look in the Mirror
Amos 1–5

 Scouting the Terrain

Amos, an 8th century prophet in the northern kingdom of Israel, begins his message with dramatic denunciations of Israel's neighbors. One by one, God calls these surrounding nations onto the carpet for terrible transgressions. Most have been behaving like bullies; Judah, for its part, is charged not with violence but with succumbing to idolatry.

Trailblazers
• God
• Amos

We can imagine Amos' audience nodding in approval, saying, "Preach it!" But then the prophet zeroes in on Israel. The nation's social injustice, idol worship, and sexual immorality have inflamed God's anger; and God makes a stinging accusation: "You only have I known of all the families of the earth; therefore I will punish you" (3:2).

God holds God's people to high standards. We Christians believe that God has, through Jesus, adopted us into God's chosen family. Sharing that relationship means sharing its responsibilities. As the apostle Peter later declares, judgment begins with the household of God (1 Peter 4:17).

• What special responsibilities are part of a relationship with God?

• When are you tempted to judge others more harshly than you judge yourself? Why?

Pace Pusher
Memorize Amos 5:14. Recite it for your Race Director.

 NOW READ AMOS 1–5.

³ Switchback

As Christians, we pray for Jesus' return, just as the people of Amos's day looked forward to "the day of the LORD." The prophet, however, cautions us as much as he cautioned his original audience that God's final intervention in history will be a day of judgment against sin. In fact, so far from being "light," it is a day of "darkness" (5:18). This is what you're waiting for? he asks.

When we pray for the day of the Lord, we must be praying, not that "others" will "get what's coming to them," but that all people, including ourselves, will at last live in the justice and righteousness that God intends (5:24).

• How comfortable are you praying for God's justice on earth? What about your life would have to change if God's justice were to become a reality?

• What changes in your life can you make today in anticipation of the coming day of the Lord Jesus?

Who says that the Bible's words aren't applicable to modern-day life? A famous leader quoted passages from the minor prophets in a famous speech. The passages are found in Isaiah 40 and Amos 5. Study the chapters, then find video clips or transcripts of the famous speech online. Go to *www.amazingbiblerace.com* and blog about your impressions of the speech and how the speaker used the Bible verses.

Road Signs

• **Cleanness of teeth:** God has sent a famine on the land as a warning. The people have "cleanness of teeth" because there is so little food to eat (and no toothbrushes).

• **"For three transgressions ... and for four":** This expression, which appears 8 times in Amos, means "For way too many transgressions."

 Prayer

Mighty God, may your justice and righteousness flow to your world through us. Amen.

When a Stranger Points the Way
Amos 6–9

1 **Scouting the Terrain**

It's like a moment out of an old Hollywood western: The local sheriff squints his eyes, sizes up the do-gooding hero, and drawls, "You ain't from around here, are ya?" Amos is from Judah but is working in Israel. Amaziah accuses Amos of meddling (7:10-17) and tells him that he should go back where he belongs and stay out of affairs that are not his business.

Sometimes only an outsider can speak the truth. People living in a wealthy nation may not be aware of their greed and materialism until someone from a poorer land points it out. A group of friends may not realize that they are excluding others until someone outside the group tells them.

God came to the world as the ultimate outsider (see John 1:10); and our challenge is to hear those who "ain't from around here" before it's too late—as it was for Amaziah.

• When have you heard God's truth through an "outsider"?

Trailblazers

• **God**
• **Amos**
• **Amaziah**
• **King Jeroboam**

• How can you develop your ability to see God in and hear God through those who are different from you?

Don't forget to enter Amos's "stats" on your Minor League Prophets Scorecard.

hurdle

2 **NOW READ AMOS 6–9.**

3 Switchback

The Church of the Holy Trinity, in Philadelphia, has a lectern carved in the shape of a standing angel. The angel's wings form the place where the large Bible rests, but the solemn look on the angel's face could be interpreted as one of difficult endurance—for good reason! As Amaziah told Jeroboam, God's Word can be hard to bear (7:10). Yet as Amos knew, we need that vulnerability and accountability before God so that we can truly live. In some ways, the famine and drought that plagued Israel (4:6-7) would be easier than the famine and drought "of hearing the words of the LORD" (8:11-12). God's Word judges us, but God's Word also saves us.

• When do you find God's Word hard to bear? What do you then do?

Pace Pusher

Money matters (8:4-7): Abusive exploitation of the poor is bad enough—but for God's chosen ones to be the abusers? Unacceptable! Amos characterizes the people as itching to get out of the pews so that they can continue to swindle those who already have so little. Instead of helping only themselves, God's people must help others.

4 Prayer

God, move us to love the poor, warn the proud, and worship you in humility and honesty. Amen.

With a Brother Like That, Who Needs Enemies?
Obadiah

1 Scouting the Terrain

As anyone who is a sibling can tell you, brothers and sisters don't always stick up for one another. When Babylon conquered Jerusalem in 587 B.C., Edom, an ancient nation in what is now southern Israel and Jordan, might have been expected to help out. After all, Edomites were descended from Esau, Jacob's elder brother.

Trailblazers
- **God**
- **Obadiah**

Unfortunately, Edom cheered on the invaders (verses 11-12). The psalmist rages, "Remember, O LORD, against the Edomites the day of Jerusalem's fall, how they said, 'Tear it down! Tear it down! Down to the foundations!' " (Psalm 137:7). Are you feeling the love?

Obadiah's book is not only the shortest in the Hebrew Bible but also the angriest. Then again, if you've ever been betrayed by someone you love—or, at least, who you thought should love you—you might not want to say much, either. And what you did say might make people uncomfortable at your next family reunion.

WEEK
10
◇
DAY
4

• Have you ever felt betrayed by a close friend or family member? How did you handle it?

Don't forget to enter Obadiah's "stats" on your Minor League Prophets Scorecard.

2

NOW READ OBADIAH.

3 Switchback

According to Obadiah, Edom's pride will lead to its destruction. That nation mistakes the mountains in which it is situated for the heights of heaven itself. But God checks that overconfidence: "Though you soar aloft like the eagle, though your nest is set among the stars, from there I will bring you down" (verse 4).

Obadiah insists that all nations are under God and that "the day of the LORD is near against" them all (verse 15). As we learned from Amos, a nation under God is not excused for its offenses against God; and Edom's greatest sin is its inflated ego, which leads to a self-centered refusal to aid a weaker nation. Obadiah's message may have important implications for wealthy and powerful nations today. Will we engage the world in arrogance or humility?

• In what ways do nations mistreat one another today?

• How can wealthy and powerful nations do a better job of humbly assisting less privileged countries?

Obadiah

4 Prayer

God, when your day dawns, may we be found humbly and faithfully following your ways. Amen.

God's Audacious Grace
Jonah 1–4

1 Scouting the Terrain

Heather Mercer and Dayna Curry, two young American relief workers, made headlines in 2001 when American and Northern Alliance troops freed them from prison in Kabul, Afghanistan, where they'd been held on charges of preaching Christianity in defiance of the Taliban's strict Islamic laws. Despite Mercer's harsh experience in a country that many viewed as America's enemy after September 11, 2001, she declared that she felt called to return to that land and its people.

Trailblazers
• God
• Jonah
• People of Nineveh
• Big fish

Jonah was no Heather Mercer! When God called him to preach a message of repentance in Nineveh, the capital of the Assyrian empire—a long-time enemy of Israel—Jonah wanted no part of it (see 4:1-3). But God has a plan to redeem Nineveh, and three days inside a giant fish convince Jonah to accept God's call. This "good news" is bad news for Jonah, who is much more interested in seeing the Assyrians punished by God than in drawing them to repent.

• When you are honest with yourself, whom do you have trouble believing, in your gut, that God could ever love?

• How can Christians contribute in practical ways to an attitude of love and goodwill toward those our society views as "the enemy"?

Don't forget to enter Jonah's "stats" on your Minor League Prophets Scorecard.

2 NOW READ JONAH 1–4.

③ Switchback

In the Gospels, Jesus actually compares himself to Jonah: He said that no sign would be given to those in his generation who did not believe in him except "the sign of Jonah" (Matthew 12:39; 16:4). Just as Jonah spent "three days and three nights" in the fish's belly before being vomited out, so would Jesus rise from the grave on the third day. Some early Christians, when teaching about how Jesus' death saves us from sin, explained that Satan overconfidently "swallowed" Jesus, only to have to "spit him out" on Easter because Jesus proved too strong for him to take!

Road Signs

• **Nineveh:** This capital of Assyria was located near what is today Mosul, Iraq.
• **Tarshish:** The location of this sea port is unknown. After hearing God's call to go to Nineveh, Jonah heads in the opposite direction.

• How would you respond if God called you to preach repentance to a vicious enemy — say, the leaders of Al Qaeda? If they repented, could you forgive?

Jonah

 Study the Book of Jonah alongside Matthew 12:38-42 and Luke 11:29-32. How are these passages related? Go to *amazingbiblerace.com* to take a quiz to see what you've learned.

Water Break

You're almost halfway through the Minor Prophets. Hang in there and keep reading about God's word to the people of the past *and* to us.

Prayer

God, may we joyfully announce your grace to all people. Amen.

How the Mighty Have Fallen
Micah 1–3

1. Scouting the Terrain

Micah, a prophet in Judah in the 8th century B.C., sees sin as a slow-spreading cancer. It worked its way from the northern kingdom into the southern, eventually reaching Jerusalem, even into the very house of God. The people of Judah had long believed Jerusalem to be invulnerable to attack because God dwelled in the Temple and would protect the city. In the end, however, that stronghold fell, as did Samaria before it. And the enemies that these cities could not withstand weren't really Assyrian or Babylonian. The true enemies were the idolatry and social evils that God's people committed, which had weakened society from within.

But God promises a restoration (2:12-13). Just as radiation and chemotherapy kill cells of the body in order cure it from cancer, the harsh punishment of the scattered remnant of God's people will eventually bring about restoration.

Trailblazers
- God
- Micah

• When have you seen something bad coming and have felt powerless to prevent it? How does that experience compare with the situation Micah describes?

• How are you sometimes your own worst enemy?

2. NOW READ MICAH 1–3.

3 Switchback

According to Micah's prophecy, sinners in Israel and Judah have fallen prey to disobedient self-centeredness: "When the morning dawns, they perform it, because it is in their power" (2:1b). In the New Testament, Paul later warns against such behavior, saying, "Do not use your freedom as an opportunity for self-indulgence" (Galatians 5:13). When we make a decision, we must ask ourselves whether our choice glorifies God and brings good to our neighbors or it is a decision made in vain to satisfy our desires.

- When have you chosen to do something just because you could? What happened?

Road Signs

- **Micah:** This name is an abbreviated form of the name Micaiah, which means, "Who is like the LORD?"
- **Moresheth:** This was Micah's hometown, a small farming village southwest of Jerusalem.
- **"Cut off your hair"** (1:16): To cut one's hair was a ritual of mourning.
- **Jacob** (2:12 and 3:9): Prophets often referred to the people of Israel and Judah as Jacob, who was their ancestor.

- When have you done the right thing even though you didn't want to do it? What happened?

Micah

4 Prayer

Lord, fill us with power and might to do justice. Amen.

109

A Two-Faced Nation
Micah 4–7

1 Scouting the Terrain

Most biblical prophets are "two-faced," gazing behind and peering ahead at the same time. Micah, for example, calls on God's people to remember the grace they have received in days gone by in their deliverance from slavery and their blessing from Balaam. If they will look in their rearview mirror, the people will recognize how far they have come, and by whose power they have done so. Unfortunately, the people have chosen to hang on to a different piece of their past: "the statutes of Omri and all the works of the house of Ahab" (6:16), quite possibly the most corrupt, most idolatrous dynasty ever to sit on Israel's throne (see 1 Kings 16:25-33).

Trailblazers

- **God**
- **Micah**

So God points the people's eyes toward the future. In the short term, the future holds judgment; but ultimately God will again work wonders, gathering scattered exiles together under the rule of a shepherd-king from the backwater town of Bethlehem (5:2-5a).

Christians today also have reason to be "two-faced." We remember how Jesus fulfilled Micah's words even as we continue doing the work of God's kingdom in anticipation of Jesus' final victory.

- How do you remember the past and, at the same time, look to the future as you serve God?

Pace Pusher

- Memorize Micah 7:7 and recite it for your Race director.

2 NOW READ MICAH 4–7.

3 Switchback

Micah 6:8 expresses what faith in God looks like. Many Christian commentators have compared Micah's declaration to Jesus' simple summary of God's Law in Matthew 22:37-40. Of course, putting Micah and Jesus' simple formulations into practice is not always so simple. But that is why our faith grows out of our relationship with God, who is always with us, to guide us as we strive to do justice, love mercy, and walk humbly.

Road Signs

- **Seven shepherds, maybe eight** (5:5): These "seven shepherds and eight installed as rulers"—the numbers are a Hebrew poetic device and not a precise head count—will rise up from the people as defenders who will conquer Babylon the conqueror.
- **"Wicked scales and a bag of dishonest weights"** (6:11): Through Micah, God accuses merchants of cheating their customers by not giving them all of the goods they pay for. In God's sight, such economic dishonesty is little different than outright violence (6:12).

- Recite Micah 6:8 to yourself several times. What specific action or attitude is God leading you to take today in response to Micah's words? In what particular ways can you do justice, love mercy, and walk humbly with God?

Micah

4 Prayer

Lord, you are always faithful to us. By your Spirit, may we faithfully do justice, love mercy, and walk humbly with you. Amen.

Don't forget to enter Micah's "stats" on your Minor League Prophets Scorecard.

hurdle

Don't Mess With YHWH
Nahum 1–3

Scouting the Terrain

Trailblazers

- **God**
- **Nahum**

The name Nahum (NAY-huhm) means "comfort"; but his words don't, at first, sound very comforting. Yet the 7th century B.C. prophet Nahum, with his brutal images, forces us to face a fact that we might overlook in longer, more eloquent prophecies. The God of the whole world is the God of Israel.

God made a once-and-for-all commitment to this otherwise minor nation. Nahum leaves no doubt that, when people mess with Israel—as Assyria frequently did—they mess with Yahweh, "slow to anger but great in power" (1:3). God will fight for Israel against those who seek to tear it apart—even as Israel, as the other prophets tell us, is "tearing up" God's heart through its sin.

As Christians, we are aware of our sins against God. Yet we find comfort knowing that nothing, not even sin, can separate us from God's love in Christ (see Romans 8:38-39).

- When, in your experience, have family ties proved stronger than anger or disappointment?

- How comforting do you find the truth that God has made a commitment of love to you that will never change?

NOW READ NAHUM 1–3.

WEEK

11

DAY

3

Switchback

Remember that these prophets' books originally circulated independently of one another. When placed together in the Bible, these texts begin a kind of "conversation" with one another—sometimes confirming and sometimes critiquing one another.

For example, while we want to understand Nahum's national pride, we also want to remember the lesson of Obadiah. Standing by to gloat as a nation meets its doom is not acceptable in God's sight.

Or consider Jonah's experience: He watched petulantly as God pardoned the very same nation that Nahum envisions being buried in a bloodbath.

Perhaps the best words Christians can take from Nahum are those similar to Isaiah 52:7: "Look! On the mountains the feet of one who brings good tidings, who proclaims peace!" (Nahum 1:15). Jesus, the Prince of Peace (remember Micah 5:5 and Isaiah 9:6) summons us to speak and live out God's peace in the middle of a violent world.

- What specific thing you can do today to be "one who brings good tidings, who proclaims peace" (Nahum 1:15)?

Road Signs

- **Mantelet** (2:5): This was a portable screen or shield that protected besieging soldiers.
- **Bashan and Carmel** (1:4): These areas were famous for their lush pastures.

Prayer

God Our Comfort, may we comfort a seriously wounded world with the good news of your love. Amen.

Don't forget to enter Nahum's "stats" on your Minor League Prophets Scorecard.

Nahum

Habakkuk's Trust Fall
Habakkuk 1–3

1 Scouting the Terrain

Trailblazers
- God
- Habukkuk

Remember the scene in *Finding Nemo* in which Marlin and Dory are inside the whale's mouth? Dory is trying to convince Marlin to surrender to the rushing waters that will carry them into the Sydney harbor. Marlin is too terrified to believe Dory's assurances that letting go is the right thing to do, partly because it was the only option they had left.

Letting go was also Habakkuk's last option. Living in Judah in the late 7th or early 6th century B.C., he watches the Babylonian Empire grow in power and size. He worries about violence and can't understand why God allows it to continue. God's first answer doesn't satisfy: God actually intends to use the brutal Babylonians. Habakkuk thinks that such scheming is beneath the Holy One of Israel (1:13). God tells Habakkuk to let go and trust.

WEEK 11 ◇ DAY 4

Maybe that answer doesn't fully persuade us, either. But what other options do we have? We can rant against all that's wrong in a wicked world; or we can offer our ranting and worrying to God and then move on, continuing to do the work God gives, trusting God to make sure that goodness and justice finally carry the day.

• How do you define *faith*?

• What have you read in the Bible so far that gives you the assurance that goodness and justice will ultimately prevail?

Don't forget to enter Habakkuk's "stats" on your Minor League Prophets Scorecard.

2 NOW READ HABAKKUK 1–3.

3 Switchback

Like Job before him, Habakkuk demonstrates that questioning God can be an important part of maturing in faith. Twice the prophet demands an explanation from God; and he settles in to wait until God provides one: "I will stand at my watchpost....I will keep watch to see what [God] will say to me" (2:1). Also like Job, Habakkuk doesn't exactly get an explanation. But God's response is enough to sustain his faith. It even causes him to break into a song of irrational joy (3:17-19).

To experience that kind of joy and trust in God for yourself, take a cue from Habakkuk. If you have a question for God, ask it. You might not get the answer you want, but you will leave yourself open to a new experience of God's presence.

• What question(s) do you have for God?

Road Sign

• **Habakkuk** (huh-BAK-uhk)**:** This name means, according to some sources, "embrace," which is appropriate because Habakkuk had to have felt fully embraced by God to stay faithful during a troubling time of doubt.

 Habakkuk 2:4 became the primary biblical support for Paul's doctrine of justification by faith. Search Paul's letters (Romans through Titus) to find two references to this Scripture. Link this Scripture also to a prominent person from Genesis. When your research is complete, take a quiz online at *amazingbiblerace.com.*

 Prayer

Lord, give us strength, patience, and faith to watch for your will. Amen.

Against Practical Atheists
Zephaniah 1–3

1 Scouting the Terrain

Practical atheism—living as though God is not watching us—has plagued God's people since biblical times. The 7th century B.C. prophet Zephaniah speaks against "those who say in their hearts, 'The LORD will not do good, nor will [God] do harm' " (1:12). Whatever these people may say with their lips, their lives demonstrate an attitude that they can do anything they please because God doesn't really care. To them, for all intents and purposes, God isn't real.

Trailblazers
• God
• Zephaniah

Zephaniah insists that God cares enough even to angrily destroy the whole earth (1:2-3, 18; 3:8). The prophet passionately calls the people to repentance before time runs out. Only the meek, who humbly trust in and live lives pleasing to God, will inherit the earth after God's cleansing judgment (3:12).

• How effectively do you think fear motivates people to believe in God?

WEEK
11
◆
DAY
5

• When have you been guilty of "practical atheism"?

hurdle Don't forget to enter Zephaniah's "stats" on your Minor League Prophets Scorecard.

2 NOW READ ZEPHANIAH 1–3.

③ Switchback

The half-century preceding Zephaniah's prophecy may have fulfilled Amos's (8:11-2) and Micah's (3:7) predictions of God's silence. King Manasseh (muh-NAS-uh) has gone down in history as one of Judah's worst monarchs. Scripture reports that Manasseh "shed very much innocent blood"—including that of his own sons, whom he sacrificed to idols (2 Kings 21:16). Two years after Manasseh's death, however, 8-year-old Josiah ascended the throne; and Judah's religious life experienced a dramatic renewal. During Josiah's reign, the priest Hilkiah found the long-lost book of God's Law in the Temple. Josiah celebrated the first Passover Judah had seen in a long time, purged idols from the land, and called on his subjects to live up to their sacred covenant to God (see 2 Kings 22–23).

Through the prophet Zephaniah, God again speaks, summoning the nation to embrace Josiah's reformation (2:3).

• When have you experienced God's silence? How, if yet, has that silence been broken?

④ Prayer

God, purify us from all pride and complacency that we may rejoice with our whole heart in your justice and love. Amen.

Water Break

Pause, take a few deep breaths, and get ready for the final week of this leg and the final books of the Old Testament.

Road Signs

• **Milcom** (1:5): Otherwise known as Molech, this was a Canaanite deity, a fire god to whom children were sacrificed.
• **The Fish Gate** (1:10): This was one of the ancient entrances to the city of Jerusalem, where the city's elite probably lived.

A Homeless Deity?
Haggai 1–2

Scouting the Terrain

Has procrastination ever gotten you into trouble? Putting things off made life hard for the exiles who came from Babylon. When God's word comes to Haggai (HAG-igh), some time after the exiles had returned to Judah; and things are again looking grim. Why? While the returnees live in nice houses, God's house lies in ruins, Haggai says.

Trailblazers
- **God**
- **Haggai**
- **King Darius**
- **Zerubbabel**
- **Joshua**

The people's decision to put off rebuilding the Temple reveals a decision to put off restoring the holy covenant relationship. In the face of the pressing realities of resettlement, the proper worship of God has been placed on the back burner indefinitely.

Most of us today lead fast-paced, overscheduled lives. With so much we want and have to do, we find it easy to push our relationship with God to the side. However, Haggai reminds us: Worship is not luxury but a necessity. When we put God first, the rest of life falls into place.

• How do you put off God in your life?

• What have you been meaning to do for God that you can start doing now?

• What do you think is "proper worship" of God? Why?

Don't forget to enter Haggai's "stats" on your Minor League Prophets Scorecard.

NOW READ HAGGAI 1–2.

3 Switchback

Haggai introduces us to two key leaders of the postexilic community: Governor Zerubbabel (zuh-RUHB-uh-buhl) and high priest Joshua. These men embody the continuation of God's people—and God's promises.

Temple-building was a monarch's job. But neither Zerubbabel nor Joshua was regarded as king. The exalted title the prophet Zechariah gives them is "sons of [anointing] oil" (4:14); Haggai writes that Zerubbabel will be God's "signet ring" (2:23). This distinction may signal the people's readiness to acclaim God alone as king.

- The apocryphal (not in the Bible) Book of Ecclesiasticus, also known as Sirach, (49:11-12) numbers Joshua and Zerubbabel as among the "famous men," heroes of faith who are worthy of praise. Who are famous men and women of faith you have personally known and consider praiseworthy? Why?

Road Sign

- **Signet ring:** This ring (2:23) bears a personal symbol, often of a king. It could be used, with wax, as a seal or a stamp of approval.

Haggai

4 Prayer

God, grant us your strength, and make us your messengers to the world. Amen.

fast forward With your team, choose a social issue about which you are concerned. Select passages from at least three of the "minor prophets" that you believe can communicate God's word about the chosen issue. Once you have identified your social issue and prophetic texts, combine them into an audio-visual presentation for your congregation. Upload your project at *amazingbiblerace.com* for points.

Pace Pusher

Sing or recite the words to the hymn "Sanctuary" (You can find words to the hymn online on sites that play the music as well. Just search for the following key words: *hymn sanctuary*.) How does this song add to your appreciation of Haggai's message?

119

Rome Wasn't Built in a Day
Zechariah 1–6

1 Scouting the Terrain

You may have heard the adage, "The journey of a thousand miles begins with one step." Zechariah, who lived in late 6th-century B.C. Judah, would have agreed with its sentiment. The visions he receives and reports are meant to help people recognize and rejoice in God's work, even if that work takes a long time.

As Haggai observed, the former exiles had heard stories of the Temple at the height of its grandeur. The new Temple must not have looked as if it would ever measure up. Many probably threw up their hands in disgust: "Our holiest place is a wreck. We'll never be what we were."

Zechariah's visions communicate God's pledge, "I will come and dwell in your midst" (2:10). What's more, God will raise up the "Branch"—the Messiah, the priest-king who will rule in glory (see 6:12-13). The Judeans are taking that first, small step on the long journey toward the fulfillment of all God's good promises.

Trailblazers

- **God**
- **Zechariah**
- **Angel of the Lord**
- **Joshua**
- **Zerubbabel**

• When have you had to start a task or project that you knew would take a long time to complete? How easy or difficult was taking the first step?

2 NOW READ ZECHARIAH 1–6.

③ Switchback

When the earliest "Christians"—all of whom, of course, identified themselves as Jews—sought to defend their claim that Jesus was the Messiah, they turned to their Scriptures for support. Zechariah provided quite a lot. For example, God's declaration, in 6:12-13, that the "Branch" to come will rule as both a priest and a king dovetails nicely with two of the titles the New Testament bestows on Jesus (for example, see Hebrews 5:5 and Revelation 19:16).

This vision of the Branch would have had a much different meaning to Zechariah's original audience. For them this oracle was a promise that a great and holy ruler will rebuild the Temple and sit on the throne in Jerusalem?

• Who or what gives you hope for the future?

• How can you use what you've learned from Scripture to give others hope for the future?

Road Sign

• **Zechariah:** This name means "The LORD remembers." Appropriately enough, Zechariah's prophecy begins as God reminds the Judeans of the problems that led their nation into exile, urging them not to repeat past mistakes.

Zechariah

 Zechariah receives eight visions in these chapters. Outline these chapters, doing your best to decode and understand the symbolism and meaning for God's people. Once you've studied the visions, take the quiz at *amazingbiblerace.com*.

④ Prayer

God, we are glad that you came to live among us in Jesus Christ, and that you dwell among us still through your Spirit. May we respond in hope and courage. Amen.

A Leader Fit for Divine Office
Zechariah 7–11

1 Scouting the Terrain

Think back to any recent political campaign. How often did questions of leadership come up? How much time (and money) did the candidates spend on bumper stickers, kissing babies, and negative ads? How much energy did they devote to grappling with hard questions of what qualities a good leader needs? How did they demonstrate (or fail to demonstrate) that they possess those qualities?

Through Zechariah, God has harsh words for bad leaders. God's criticism for bad leaders suggests that good leaders exhibit compassion, foresight, diligence, and a nourishing and healing nature.

And why shouldn't God demand these traits? For they are all qualities God possesses. Christians see that truth nowhere clearer than in the life of Jesus, who, on the first Palm Sunday, came to his people "triumphant and victorious" yet "humble and riding on a donkey" (Zechariah 9:9). God has every right to expect that leaders will love "their" people, for they and "their" people all belong to God.

Trailblazers

• **God**
• **Zechariah**
• **Sharezer**
• **Ragem-melech**
• **Israel's shepherds**

• What makes a good leader?

• How can you be a godly leader in your congregation? in your school? in your community? in your family?

2 NOW READ ZECHARIAH 7–11.

3 Switchback

Early in the 16th century, Sir Thomas More published *Utopia*. The title, which literally means "no place," has come to mean a perfect society. The renewed Jerusalem depicted in Zechariah's prophecy is a utopia (see 8:3-5 and 14:6-11). But this perfect society does not come about by human effort. It is the result of God's firm resolve "to do good to Jerusalem" (8:15), a decision just as firm now as was the decision to punish it in the past.

God's mind is made up: "I will return to Zion" (8:3). God uses Zechariah to paint a word picture of what is possible for God but impossible for mortals. A utopian future is too good to be true if only sinful humans are involved. But when God is on the scene, nothing is impossible.

- What is something that seems impossible to you but would not be impossible to God?

Road Signs

- **Teraphim** (TER-uh-fihm) (10:2): These were statues or other images of household idols, such as those Rachel stole from her father in Genesis 31. Here God commands people to stop relying on such "utter nonsense" and to, instead, ask for rain from the rain's true source.
- **Authentic worship** (7:1-10): When God's people ask whether they should continue to fast as they did while in exile, God reminds them that real worship consists of inner integrity and outward justice.

4 Prayer

Lord, we offer our lives to you, praying that your Spirit will empower us to live with mercy and compassion, love and truthfulness, with hearts pleasing to you. Amen.

What's to Be Done With a Violent God?
Zechariah 12–14

1 Scouting the Terrain

Trailblazers

- **God**
- **Zechariah**

Disturbingly violent scenes fill these final chapters: the nations marching to strike Jerusalem, only to be struck themselves and made virtual zombies; parents stabbing their prophesying children; homes robbed, women attacked. What's most disturbing is that God sets it all in motion. Zechariah envisions a future in which Judah wins and everyone else loses.

No amount of historical context can explain the violence away. But we need to remember that Israel and Judah had been pushed around by powerful neighboring empires for centuries. As 21st-century citizens of a wealthy and powerful nation, we might find it difficult to take the point of view of a perpetual underdog. Think of a time when you have been bullied. Imagine that bullying was all you ever knew. You'd rejoice to learn that God planned to fight on your side.

WEEK 12 ◆ DAY 4

• How do you react to Zechariah's portrayal of God's violence?

• How does living in a prosperous and powerful nation shape how you read Scripture?

• What images would you choose to describe God's ultimate rule over the earth? Why?

2 NOW READ ZECHARIAH 12–14.

3 Switchback

Zechariah's final vision of God's coming future shaped the way Jesus' first followers interpreted their experience of God in his life, death, and resurrection. For example, the anonymous shepherd who is struck in 13:7 is taken to be Jesus (Matthew 26:31). The obscure discussion of the pierced one in 12:10 anticipates the blood and water that pours from Jesus' pierced side at his crucifixion (John 19:37). Jesus becomes the source of the fountain that cleanses from sin (Zechariah 13:1).

In an effort to show how the prophets point to Jesus, however, we Christian readers may overlook other aspects of these texts. In the case of the widespread wailing, for example, notice that the "spirit of compassion and supplication" is a gift from God (12:10). A nation that wails and weeps for those killed in battle, including its "enemies," demonstrates that God has given the nation a sense of how precious life is.

Road Sign
• **Mount of Olives** (14:4): This is a ridge east of Jerusalem. In large part because of Zechariah's prophecy that it will be the location from which God starts the divine rule of the world "on that day," many Jews from ancient times have desired burial there. The Garden of Gethsemane, the site of Jesus' arrest, is at the mount's foot.

• Whom do you know of who has followed the example of the "pierced one" by suffering for the good of the community, nation, or world?

• When have you felt sympathy or compassion for someone whom you considered an enemy?

hurdle Don't forget to enter Zechariah's "stats" on your Minor League Prophets Scorecard.

4 Prayer

God, you have made us holy to you. May we show your holiness to all the world. Amen.

Zechariah

Faithful Actions Speak Louder Than Words
Malachi 1–4

1 Scouting the Terrain

As Malachi begins his prophetic ministry, some of the lessons of the exile seem to be wearing off. Priests are bringing substandard offerings to the altar of God (1:7-9). Men are breaking faith with their wives and with God (2:10-16). Society's poor and vulnerable are being exploited (3:5b). People are abandoning what is good in favor of what is easy; after all, they say, we can get away with all sorts of wild and wicked stuff (3:14-15).

Trailblazers

• **God**
• **Malachi**

Malachi takes up the refrain we heard from Amos and Hosea: The day of the Lord is coming! Repent while there's still time! "Return to me, and I will return to you, says the LORD of hosts" (3:7).

As you read Malachi, use his words to measure your own spiritual life. Are you "going through the motions"? How do you treat the people our society wants to ignore and forget? Do you usually do what's easy, or what's right?

• How many times do you have to hear something before you really "get it"?

• When have you knowingly made the same mistake over and over? What happened?

Don't forget to enter Malachi's "stats" on your Minor League Prophets Scorecard.

2 NOW READ MALACHI 1–4.

In Christian Bibles, Malachi's prophecy forms the end of the Old Testament. Its position, just a few pages before the beginning of Matthew, invites us to see how the events of Jesus' birth, life, and death meet some of the very expectations Malachi raises. Most notably, God's promise to send Elijah in advance of the day of the Lord anticipates the appearance of John the Baptist, who preached about the cleansing fire of God.

The Jewish Bible, the Tanakh (TAH-nahk), contains the same writings in our Old Testament and is divided into three parts: Torah, Prophets, and Writings. Malachi is the last part of a larger book called the Twelve Prophets, which is the final book in Prophets. Writings, the third section, follows, ending with Chronicles and Cyrus's conquest of Babylon (2 Chronicles 36:22-23). The Jewish arrangement of books underscores the endless possibility of renewal that God offers. In fact, when Jews read Malachi publicly, they repeat 4:5 after 4:6 in order to end with the hope that faith in God brings.

• Why, do you think, did Christians choose Malachi as the final book of the Old Testament?

Road Sign

• **The covenant with Levi** (2:4-9; 3:3-4): The tribe of Levi, who descended from Jacob's third son, was selected by God to be the tribe from which priests would be drawn.

Malachi

Leg 4 Finish Line

WOO-HOO! You did it! You've finished the Old Testament! It was tough at times, but you kept going!

Now, take a big breath and get ready for Leg 5 of the AMAZING BIBLE RACE, where you will read about Jesus: his life, his teachings, his death, and his resurrection.

---

4 **Prayer**

Hail the heaven-born Prince of Peace! Hail the Sun of Righteousness! Light and life to all he brings, risen with healing in his wings.
—Charles Wesley, from "Hark! The Herald Angels Sing"

AMAZING BIBLE RACE
Team Covenant

As a member of _____
(Team Name)

in The Amazing Bible Race, I make this covenant to read my daily

Bible readings, read my Runner's Reader, and answer the reflection

questions. I commit to supporting my teammates and being held

accountable by them for doing all I can do to make the most of this

experience. I will be present at team meetings and youth group.

I am determined to grow in my knowledge of God's Word in my

personal faith journey.

_____   _____
(Signature)   (Date)

Have team members sign below and put their contact information
(e-mail address, phone numbers, text addresses, and IM names) nearby.